LifeChange

A NAVPRESS BIBLE S

*A life-changing
encounter with God's Word*

2 CORINTHIANS

*Paul defends the gospel by placing
both himself and the Corinthians under
the authority of Jesus Christ.*

NavPress

A NavPress resource published in alliance
with Tyndale House Publishers, Inc.

NavPress is the publishing ministry of The Navigators, an international Christian organization and leader in personal spiritual development. NavPress is committed to helping people grow spiritually and enjoy lives of meaning and hope through personal and group resources that are biblically rooted, culturally relevant, and highly practical.

For more information, visit www.NavPress.com.

CONTENTS

ACKNOWLEDGMENTS

The LIFECHANGE series has been produced through the coordinated efforts of a team of Navigator Bible study developers and NavPress editorial staff, along with a nationwide network of field-testers.

AUTHOR: TED DORMAN
SERIES EDITOR: KAREN LEE-THORP

HOW TO USE THIS STUDY

Objectives

Most guides in the LIFECHANGE series of Bible studies cover one book of the Bible. Although the LIFECHANGE guides vary with the books they explore, they share some common goals:

1. To provide you with a firm foundation of understanding and a thirst to return to the book.

2. To teach you by example how to study a book of the Bible without structured guides.

3. To give you all the historical background, word definitions, and explanatory notes you need, so that your only other reference is the Bible.

4. To help you grasp the message of the book as a whole.

5. To teach you how to let God's Word transform you into Christ's image.

Each lesson in this study is designed to take sixty to ninety minutes to complete on your own. The guide is based on the assumption that you are completing one lesson per week, but if time is limited you can do half a lesson per week or whatever amount allows you to be thorough.

Flexibility

LIFECHANGE guides are flexible, allowing you to adjust the quantity and depth of your study to meet your individual needs. The guide offers many optional questions in addition to the regular numbered questions. The optional questions, which appear in the margins of the study pages, include the following:

Optional Application. Nearly all application questions are optional; we hope you will do as many as you can without overcommitting yourself.

For Thought and Discussion. Beginning Bible students should be able to handle these, but even advanced students need to think about them. These questions frequently deal with ethical issues and other biblical principles. They often offer cross-references to spark thought, but the references do not give obvious answers. They are good for group discussions.

For Further Study. These include: (a) cross-references that shed light on a topic the book discusses, and (b) questions that delve deeper into the passage. You can omit them to shorten a lesson without missing a major point of the passage.

If you are meeting in a group, decide together which optional questions to prepare for each lesson, and how much of the lesson you will cover at the next meeting. Normally, the group leader should make this decision, but you might let each member choose his or her own application questions.

As you grow in your walk with God, you will find the LIFECHANGE guide growing with you—a helpful reference on a topic, a continuing challenge for application, a source of questions for many levels of growth.

Overview and details

The study begins with an overview of 2 Corinthians. The key to interpretation is context—what is the whole passage or book *about?*—and the key to context is purpose—what is the author's *aim* for the whole work? In lesson 1 you will lay the foundation for your study of 2 Corinthians by asking yourself, *Why did the author (and God) write the book? What did they want to accomplish? What is the book about?*

In lessons 2 through 13, you will analyze successive passages of 2 Corinthians in detail. Thinking about how a paragraph fits into the overall goal of the book will help you to see its purpose. Its purpose will help you see its meaning. Frequently reviewing a chart or outline of the book will enable you to make these connections.

After you have completed the final lesson, you may want to review 2 Corinthians, returning to the big picture to see whether your view of it has changed after closer study. Review will also strengthen your grasp of major issues and give you an idea of how you have grown from your study.

Kinds of questions

Bible study on your own—without a structured guide—follows a progression. First you observe: What does the passage *say?* Then you interpret: What does the passage *mean?* Lastly you apply: How does this truth *affect* my life?

Some of the "how" and "why" questions will take some creative thinking, even prayer, to answer. Some are opinion questions without clear-cut right answers; these will lend themselves to discussions and side studies.

Don't let your study become an exercise in knowledge alone. Treat the passage as God's Word, and stay in dialogue with Him as you study. Pray,

"Lord, what do You want me to see here?" "Father, why is this true?" "Lord, how does this apply to my life?"

It is important that you write down your answers. The act of writing clarifies your thinking and helps you to remember.

Study aids

A list of reference materials, including a few notes of explanation to help you make good use of them, begins on page 125. This guide is designed to include enough background to let you interpret with just your Bible and the guide. Still, if you want more information on a subject or want to study a book on your own, try the references listed.

Scripture versions

The Bible quotations in this guide are from the New International Version of the Bible.

Use any translation you like for study, preferably more than one. A paraphrase such as The Living Bible is not accurate enough for study, but it can be helpful for comparison or devotional reading.

Memorizing and meditating

A psalmist wrote, "I have hidden your word in my heart that I might not sin against you" (Psalm 119:11). If you write down a verse or passage that challenges or encourages you and reflect on it often for a week or more, you will find it beginning to affect your motives and actions. We forget quickly what we read once; we remember what we ponder.

When you find a significant verse or passage, you might copy it onto a card to keep with you. Set aside five minutes during each day just to think about what the passage might mean in your life. Recite it over to yourself, exploring its meaning. Then, return to your passage as often as you can during your day, for a brief review. You will soon find it coming to mind spontaneously.

For group study

A group of four to ten people allows the richest discussions, but you can adapt this guide for other sized groups. It will suit a wide range of group types, such as home Bible studies, growth groups, youth groups, and businessmen's studies. Both new and experienced Bible students, and new and mature Christians, will benefit from the guide. You can omit or leave for later years any questions you find too easy or too hard.

The guide is intended to lead a group through one lesson per week. However, feel free to split lessons if you want to discuss them more thoroughly. Or, omit some questions in a lesson if preparation or discussion time is limited. You can always return to this guide for personal study later. You will be able to discuss only a few questions at length, so choose some for discussion and others for background. Make time at each discussion for members to ask about anything they didn't understand.

Each lesson in the guide ends with a section called "For the Group." These sections give advice on how to focus a discussion, how you might apply the lesson in your group, how you might shorten a lesson, and so on. The group leader should read each "For the Group" at least a week ahead so that he or she can tell the group how to prepare for the next lesson.

Each member should prepare for a meeting by writing answers for all of the background and discussion questions to be covered. If the group decides not to take an hour per week for private preparation, then expect to take at least two meetings per lesson to work through the questions. Application will be very difficult, however, without private thought and prayer.

Two reasons for studying in a group are accountability and support. When each member commits in front of the rest to seek growth in an area of life, you can pray with one another, listen jointly for God's guidance, help one another to resist temptation, assure each other that the other's growth matters to you, use the group to practice spiritual principles, and so on. Pray about one another's commitments and needs at most meetings. Spend the first few minutes of each meeting sharing any results from applications prompted by previous lessons. Then discuss new applications toward the end of the meeting. Follow such sharing with prayer for these and other needs.

If you write down each other's applications and prayer requests, you are more likely to remember to pray for them during the week, ask about them at the next meeting, and notice answered prayers. You might want to get a notebook for prayer requests and discussion notes.

Notes taken during discussion will help you to remember, follow up on ideas, stay on the subject, and clarify a total view of an issue. But don't let note-taking keep you from participating. Some groups choose one member at each meeting to take notes. Then someone copies the notes and distributes them at the next meeting. Rotating these tasks can help include people. Some groups have someone take notes on a large pad of paper or erasable marker board so that everyone can see what has been recorded.

Page 128 lists some good sources of counsel for leading group studies.

INTRODUCTION

Historical Background

Map of the Roman Empire

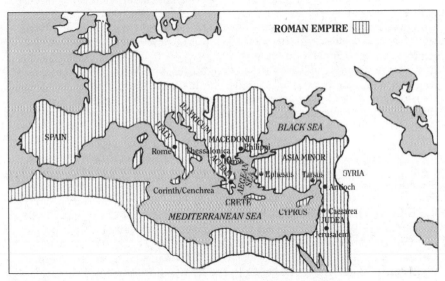

Corinth was a key economic crossroads in the ancient Mediterranean area. Located on a narrow isthmus forty-five miles southwest of Athens, Corinth had controlling access to two major seas: the Aegean to the east and the Ionian on the west. Corinth thus became a prosperous trading center first in the Greek Empire and later in the Roman one.

With its worldly wealth, Corinth also gained a well-deserved reputation for worldly ways. The worship of Corinthian Aphrodite, for example, featured a temple with 1,000 priestesses—sacred prostitutes with whom male worshipers acted out fertility rites. Needless to say, this temple was a major drawing card for the sailors who frequented the city. So rampant was this sort of behavior in Corinth that the Greeks coined a verb, *Korinthiazomai*, which meant "to live like a Corinthian in the practice of sexual immorality."

In Paul's day Corinth had a population estimated at 250,000 free persons, plus as many as 400,000 slaves. Although not an intellectual center like Athens, many of its people nevertheless were interested in Greek philosophy and placed a high premium on "wisdom" (see, for example, 1 Corinthians 1:18-31). However, the church at Corinth evidently did not contain many of these philosophy fans (see 1 Corinthians 1:26).

Most of the Christians at Corinth were probably Gentiles, even though a Jewish synagogue did exist in Corinth. In 1 Corinthians 12:2 Paul notes that on the whole, the Corinthian Christians were previously led astray to "mute idols," a phrase hardly befitting a Jewish convert.

Paul and the church at Corinth

Paul was a missionary for much of his life, both before and after his conversion to Christianity. He was a Jew by birth, but his education was far from what a normal Jew would have received. His learning encompassed not only the Pharisaic approach to the Jewish law but also the Greek disciplines of rhetoric and classical literature. As a Pharisee, he believed that God had set him apart to study and live by the Law of Moses, and like a good Pharisee, he expected a Man to arise who would liberate Israel from the grip of Roman domination. Accordingly, when some Jews began saying that Jesus (who obviously hadn't overthrown Rome) was this predicted Messiah, he stood against them with a vengeance!

In a sense, Saul (Paul's Jewish name) became a zealous anti-Christian missionary. His first appearance in the New Testament is that of a persecutor of the church of Jesus Christ. He officiated at the stoning of Stephen; he imprisoned every Christian he could get his hands on in Jerusalem; and he even made "missionary trips" to areas outside Palestine to bring back believers in Christ who had fled for safety (see Acts 7:58–8:3; 9:1-2; 1 Corinthians 15:9; Philippians 3:6). His mission was to stop the spread of Christianity.

On such a trip to Damascus, Saul had a blinding encounter with Jesus Christ. This event, which took place around AD 35, led him to turn from Pharasaism to a devoted obedience to the living and resurrected Christ. He ended up joining those he had been persecuting! Formerly he was a missionary against the church of Christ. Now he became a missionary par excellence for the cause of Christ.

Paul founded the church at Corinth around AD 51 or 52, during his second missionary journey (see Acts 18:1-17), after having passed through Macedonia (see Acts 16–17). Following his initial ministry in the city, which lasted over a year and a half (see Acts 18:11), Paul's contact with the Corinthians proceeded something like this:

1. After leaving Corinth for his first trip to Ephesus, Paul wrote a letter to the Corinthians (see 1 Corinthians 5:9; "the previous letter" is now lost to us).

2. Some time later, during his second stay in Ephesus (around AD 55), Paul wrote a second letter (our 1 Corinthians), occasioned by disturbing reports he had received from some of the Christians at Corinth.
3. That letter evidently was not sufficient to resolve the difficulties of the fledgling church, so Paul paid a personal visit to Corinth. He was later to call this a "painful visit" (2 Corinthians 2:1) since he was unable to resolve the problems there and was openly insulted by one or more opponents. These opponents may have been Corinthian Christians, but it is more likely that they were Palestinian Jews (see 2 Corinthians 11:22). Whether they were professing Christians or not we cannot be certain.
4. His authority having been openly challenged, Paul left Corinth for Ephesus and sent a letter to Corinth by the hand of his fellow worker, Titus. This "tearful" letter (now lost to us; see 2 Corinthians 2:3) called for the punishment of the one who had wronged Paul during the apostle's painful visit. In addition, Paul instructed Titus to organize a collection for the Christians in Jerusalem (see 2 Corinthians 8:6).
5. Paul continued his ministry in Ephesus, then went through Macedonia again to organize the collection on behalf of the Jerusalem church. There he met Titus, who informed him that the majority of the Corinthians had taken the admonitions of Paul's "tearful letter" to heart and had responded favorably (see 2 Corinthians 7:5-16).
6. Paul continued his evangelistic work and eventually returned to Macedonia, where he heard of fresh problems at Corinth. This, along with Paul's concern for the collection, prompted the apostle to write yet a fourth letter to the church at Corinth (our 2 Corinthians), probably before the onset of winter in AD 56.
7. Paul spent three months in Greece, primarily in Corinth (the "third visit" he mentions in 2 Corinthians 12:14 and 13:1; see Acts 20:2-3). During this time he probably wrote his most famous work, the letter to the Christians at Rome.

Occasion and purpose of 2 Corinthians

As the previous section suggests, two circumstances prompted Paul to send this letter to Corinth: the news from Titus that the Corinthians had taken his "tearful letter" to heart, and the arrival of fresh disturbing news about the situation at Corinth.

At the center of the controversy were those in Corinth whom Paul labeled "false apostles" (2 Corinthians 11:13). These were evidently Jews from Jerusalem who were teaching that adherence to the Law of Moses was necessary for salvation. Paul responded with a carefully crafted theological argument (see 3:1–5:21) showing the superiority of the new covenant of Christianity over the old covenant of Judaism. In addition, these false teachers were trying to usurp Paul's apostolic authority, challenging his credentials (see 3:1; 10:12-18) and exercising a domineering style of leadership over those who would follow them (see 11:20).

If the man or men who had openly humiliated Paul previously were followers of the false apostles, then it appears that the Corinthians took to heart Paul's criticisms and largely rejected these renegade teachers for a while, since Paul commends the Corinthians for having responded favorably to his "tearful letter." But Paul's opponents were evidently persistent, for Paul found it necessary to devote the last third of this letter to demolishing the arguments of the "false apostles."

Paul's purpose in writing 2 Corinthians, then, was to defend the gospel of Christ by forcefully reminding the Corinthians that what they had heard Paul preach was indeed God's truth. To do this, the apostle had to spend much time defending both his ministry (see 2:14–5:21) and his integrity, since the truth of the gospel was inextricably linked to whether or not Paul was truly an apostle of Christ. But Paul's spirited self-defense was not meant as an end in itself; rather, it was necessary in order to ensure the spiritual welfare of the Corinthian church (see 12:19).

The unity of 2 Corinthians

Even the casual reader will note a pronounced change in tone between the end of chapter 9 and the beginning of chapter 10. In 2 Corinthians 1–9 Paul, while critical of the Corinthians at points, is able to say things like "I can have complete confidence in you" (7:16). In chapters 10–13, however, he appears to see the situation in Corinth as desperate, so much so that he speaks with a forcefulness unparalleled in the earlier chapters. For this reason some scholars have posited that chapters 10–13 represent portions of a letter written either before (such as the "tearful letter") or after 2 Corinthians 1–9.

Without going into the arguments for or against the unity of 2 Corinthians, two things need to be said. First, there is absolutely no manuscript evidence indicating that 2 Corinthians was ever anything but a unified document. Second, there is enough common ground between the themes of chapters 1–9 and chapters 10–13 to argue for 2 Corinthians being a unified letter. While not unaware of the critical problems surrounding this letter, the present study guide will presuppose the unity of 2 Corinthians.

Principal themes

"God's ability revealed through human inability" is a theme that ties together the entire letter. Paul's opponents at Corinth were evidently being seduced by those who claimed powerful worldly credentials and attacked Paul as being a weakling. In reply, Paul argues that the gospel does not involve strong people doing great things for God, but rather teaches that God does great things through, and despite, our afflictions or weaknesses (see 2:16; 3:4-5; 4:7-12; 6:4-10; 10:17; 11:30; 12:7-10).

The biggest contrast between chapters 1–9 and chapters 10–13 is Paul's rhetorical boasting in the latter section, which is completely absent in the former. Why Paul added a final broadside against his opponents after dealing with them more subtly in chapters 1–9 is not clear. Perhaps he reviewed what he had dictated in chapters 1–9 and concluded that the situation at Corinth demanded stronger medicine. Or perhaps he received further news after completing chapters 1–9. In any event, the differences between the two sections of the letter are more of tone and emphasis than of substance. The basic themes and purpose remain consistent throughout this most personal of Paul's letters. His pastoral concern for the Corinthians and his absolute dependence upon the power of God shine forth like a lighthouse beacon, guiding his spiritual children past dangerous shoals that would sabotage their faith.

An outline of 2 Corinthians

I. Paul defends his conduct and apostolic ministry (1:1–7:16)
    A. Greetings and thanksgiving (1:1-11)
    B. Paul's singleness of purpose (1:12-22)
    C. Why Paul changed his plans (1:23–2:4)
    D. Discipline and forgiveness (2:5-11)
    E. On to Macedonia (2:12-13)
    F. Major digression: Apostolic ministry described
       1. Triumph of the gospel (2:14-17)
       2. Letters of the heart (3:1-3)
       3. A life-giving ministry (3:4-6)
       4. The glory of the new covenant (3:7–4:6)
          a. It brings life, not death (3:7-11)
          b. It unveils an everlasting glory (3:12-18)
          c. It enlightens our hearts (4:1-6)
       5. Priceless treasure in cracked pots (4:7–5:10)
          a. Through death to life (4:7-15)
          b. "We walk by faith, not by sight" (4:16–5:10)
       6. The ministry of reconciliation (5:11–6:2)
          a. Motivation for ministry (5:11-15)
          b. The message of reconciliation (5:16–6:2)
       7. A pastor's plea to his troubled flock (6:3–7:4)
          a. The perils of Paul (6:3-10)
          b. A plea for loyalty (6:11–7:4)
    G. Paul resumes his narrative: Salutary effects of spiritual discipline (7:5-16)
II. The collection for the saints at Jerusalem (8:1–9:15)
    A. The need for the collection (8:1-15)
    B. The work connected with the collection (8:16–9:5)
    C. The results of the collection (9:6-15)

III. Paul vindicates his apostolic authority (10:1–13:14)
   A. The power of Paul's ministry (10:1-11)
   B. The scope of Paul's ministry (10:12-18)
   C. Paul's jealousy for the Corinthians (11:1-6)
   D. Financial dependence and independence (11:7-12)
   E. False apostles (11:13-15)
   F. Playing the fool (11:16-21a)
   G. Boasting in weakness (11:21b–12:13)
      1. More perils of Paul (11:21b-33)
      2. The vision and the thorn (12:1-10)
      3. The need to be foolish (12:11-13)
   H. Final appeal, admonitions, and farewell (12:14–13:14)
      1. No burden except love (12:14-18)
      2. Fears about the unrepentant (12:19-21)
      3. A stern admonition (13:1-4)
      4. "Examine yourselves" (13:5-10)
      5. Conclusion (13:11-14)

2 CORINTHIANS 1:1-11

Overview

First impressions

The best way to get acquainted with 2 Corinthians is to read the entire letter before doing any in-depth study. This should only take you about an hour if you read quickly to gain an overall impression of Paul's message.

If your Bible has subtitles for the various sections of 2 Corinthians, use them as guides to help you catch the drift of Paul's argument. At the same time, realize that these subtitles, like chapter and verse divisions, are not part of the original text and may at times lead you in the wrong direction!

As you read, jot down answers to questions 1–3.

1. What are your first impressions about 2 Corinthians? (For example: Why did Paul write it? What are the principal themes? What impression do you get of Paul?)

   _____

   _____

   _____

   _____

   _____

2. Repetition offers a clue as to what a writer is trying to emphasize. What key words or phrases do you find repeated throughout 2 Corinthians?

_____

_____

_____

_____

_____

_____

_____

3. If you find outlining helpful, fill in the following outline with titles for the various sections. If you prefer, fill in the outline as you complete each lesson of the study guide. See detailed outline of 2 Corinthians.

1:1–7:16   Paul defends his conduct and apostolic ministry

1:1-11 _____

1:12-22 _____

1:23–2:4 _____

2:5-11 _____

2:12-13 _____

2:14–7:4   Major digression: Apostolic ministry described

2:14–3:6 _____

3:7–4:6 _____

4:7–5:10 _____

5:11–6:2 _____

6:3–7:4 _____

7:5-16   Return to Paul's narrative

7:5-16 _____

Paul's introduction (1:1-11)

Paul's introduction here follows the same basic form as his letters. The apostle expands upon the standard contemporary introduction, "greetings" (Greek *chaire*; see, for example, James 1:1), by writing "grace [*charis*] and peace to you from God our Father and the Lord Jesus Christ" (1:2). In this way he underscores two major themes in his letters: the grace of God toward sinful humanity, and the peace between God and humankind that resulted from the coming of Jesus Christ and His work of reconciliation on the cross. Paul follows by thanking God for working in the lives of both himself and his readers.

Greeting (1:1-2)

Apostle (1:1). From the Greek *apostello*, "to send"; hence, one sent to preach the gospel. In the New Testament this word refers to those who (1) had seen the risen Christ and (2) had been commissioned by Christ as authoritative spokespersons in His stead. The word may also derive from the Greek Old Testament translation of the Hebrew, meaning one who was an

17

"ambassador," or one who spoke with the full authority of the one who had sent him (see, for example, 1 Samuel 25:4-5 and 2 Samuel 10:1-2).

The fact that the New Testament apostles "saw, heard, and touched" the Word of Life (see 1 John 1:1-3) indicates that their authority in church history is unique, since by definition no one living after the time of Christ and the apostles could be an eyewitness. For this reason the church has always regarded the apostolic writings—our New Testament—as uniquely authoritative for Christian faith and conduct.

4. Paul refers to himself as an apostle "by the will of God" (1:1). State in your own words what you think Paul means by this phrase. Why do you think he emphasized it?

_____

_____

_____

_____

_____

_____

Thanksgiving (1:3-11)

5. As in all of his letters, Paul's major theme appears in this first section of 2 Corinthians. In 1:3-7, which two key concepts are consistently repeated by Paul? (A concept is represented either by one word, or by two or more words with the same basic meaning.)

_____

_____

_____

_____

6. Taken together, these two concepts display the theme of 2 Corinthians. In your own words, write in one sentence what you see as the theme of 2 Corinthians 1:3-7.

_____

_____

_____

_____

_____

_____

For Further Study: Read John 14–16. How does the Holy Spirit act as a comforter to believers?

For Thought and Discussion: Share an experience you have had in which someone else's affliction has enabled that person to be a comfort to you, or an affliction you have undergone that has enabled you to comfort someone else.

Optional Application: Pray that the Holy Spirit will be your Comforter this week in one specific area of need in your life.

Comfort (1:3-7). Both the noun ("comfort") and the verb ("comforts," "are comforted") derive from the Greek *parakealeo*. It means literally, "to call alongside" and hence, to "encourage" (Colossians 4:8), "exhort" (Acts 16:40, RSV), "console" (Matthew 2:18, RSV), and as here, "comfort." The noun form, "comforter" (*paraklesis*), is the word Jesus used when speaking of the Holy Spirit (see John 14:16,26; 15:26). It is translated "advocate" in the New International Version, and was used as a legal term meaning "counsel for the defense." The picture is one of the Spirit of Christ standing beside Christians to defend them from whatever opposition Satan might hurl at them.

---

7. How does God use "troubles" (1:4) in a Christian's life?

_____

_____

_____

_____

_____

_____

For Thought and Discussion: How does Paul's attitude toward suffering differ from the way most of us typically respond to suffering? How did Paul acquire this attitude?

For Thought and Discussion: How easy is it for you to view suffering as Paul did? Why is that? What would help you cultivate his attitude?

8. Do "the sufferings of Christ" (1:5) refer primarily to (a) the pain Christ suffered on the cross or (b) the persecutions suffered by those who follow Christ faithfully? Explain your answer. (*Note:* Paul's view of "the sufferings of Christ" was probably shaped by his encounter with Christ on the road to Damascus; see Acts 9:4-5.)

_____

_____

_____

_____

_____

_____

9. What lesson does Paul want the Corinthians to learn from the terrible "troubles" (1:8) he endured in Asia?

_____

_____

_____

_____

_____

10. How does Paul's description of God as the one "who raises the dead" (1:9) strengthen the point he is trying to make in 1:8?

_____

_____

_____

_____

_____

11. What two results does Paul see coming from the prayers of the Corinthian Christians (see 1:10-11)?

_____

_____

_____

_____

_____

For Further Study: Read Paul's first letter to the Corinthians. Make a list of themes common to 1 and 2 Corinthians.

12. Read 1:3-11 again. Does "comfort" here mean (a) consolation in affliction or (b) deliverance from affliction? Cite evidence from the text to support your choice.

_____

_____

_____

_____

_____

13. On the basis of 1:3-11, how would you characterize Paul's relationship with the Christians at Corinth?

_____

_____

_____

_____

Your response

14. What truth from 1:1-11 seems personally relevant to you today?

_____

_____

_____

_____

_____

_____

15. How will you respond to this truth?

_____

_____

_____

_____

16. List any questions you have from this overview.

_____

_____

_____

_____

_____

For the group

This "For the Group" section and the ones in later lessons are intended to suggest ways of structuring your discussions. Feel free to select what suits your group. The main goals of this first lesson are to gain a general understanding of 2 Corinthians, and to get to know the people with whom you will be studying.

If you read the entire book, this may be the most time-consuming lesson of the study. The group leader should advise members to allow between one and two hours for reading 2 Corinthians. If reading the whole book is an impossible demand on someone's time, he or she should try to get a general impression of 2 Corinthians by skimming portions of it to take note of repeated ideas.

Worship. Some groups like to begin with prayer and/or singing. Some pray only briefly for God's guidance at the beginning, and leave extended prayer until after the study.

Warm-up. The beginning of a new study is a good time to lay a foundation for honest sharing of ideas, to get comfortable with each other, and to encourage a sense of common purpose. One way to establish common ground is to talk about what each group member hopes to get out of your group—out of your study of 2 Corinthians, and out of any prayer, singing, sharing, outreach, or anything else you might do together. You can include what you hope to give to the group as well. If you have someone write down each member's hopes and expectations, then you can look back at these goals later to see if they are being met. You can then plan more time for prayer or decide to cover 2 Corinthians more slowly if necessary.

You may decide to take about fifteen minutes at the beginning of your discussion of lesson 1 to discuss goals. Or, you may prefer to take a whole meeting to hand out the study guides, introduce the study, examine the "How to Use This Study" section on pages 5–8, and discuss goals.

First impressions. From lesson 1 you should get, above all, first impressions of the book's themes and purposes on which to build deeper discoveries later. To focus your discussion, each group member might choose a section that was especially meaningful to him or her, and explain why. Ask group members to describe briefly what sort of person Paul appears to be. This open sharing could help introduce members who do not know each other well.

You probably will not feel it necessary to discuss question 3 (the outline). However, do share ideas about why Paul introduced this letter the way he did (see 1:3-11).

Application. If application is unfamiliar to some group members, choose a sample paragraph from 2 Corinthians and discuss possible ways of applying it. Try to state specifically how the passage is relevant to you and how you might act in light of it. Think of responses that you might actually do, not just ideal responses. Don't forget to emphasize that ability, courage, discipline, and guidance to do something are all appropriate to pray for when applying a passage.

Give the group a chance to voice any questions about the book or its historical background. You may decide to postpone answering some questions until you deal with the relevant passage, but you can keep a list of the group's questions.

Wrap-up. The wrap-up is a time to bring the discussion to a focused end and to make any announcements about the next lesson or meeting. For example, at the end of the present session (lesson 1), lead into lesson 2 by asking group members to ponder how Paul's remarks in 1:3-11 were meant to prepare the Corinthians for what he would say in 1:12–2:13.

Worship. Praise God for Paul's dedication to the gospel and his love for the Corinthians. Praise God also for insight to understand Paul's message and wisdom to apply it to your daily life.

2 CORINTHIANS 1:12-2:13

Paul's Change of Plans

Paul had suffered much on behalf of the Corinthian Christians, and thus felt very close to them. The relationship had been strained, however, by misunderstandings that had arisen because of a faction at Corinth that opposed Paul. Any apparent misstep by the apostle served as an occasion for these opponents to criticize him. So when he had to change his travel plans and postpone a return visit to Corinth, they made the most of it. For this reason, Paul now explained why he changed his travel plans and insisted that such a change did not mean he was fickle or uncaring toward the Corinthians.

Paul's singleness of purpose (1:12-22)

Boast (1:12). The word Paul uses here may carry the negative connotations of the English words *boast* and *brag*, but need not necessarily do so. Here Paul says specifically that his boast is a good one, since it centers on his Christlike conduct and consideration for the Corinthians. In other places Paul boasts of his readers' faithfulness to Christ (see 1:14), and especially of God's faithfulness to His people. "Let the one who boasts boast in the Lord" (1 Corinthians 1:31; 2 Corinthians 10:17). The sort of boasting which Paul condemns is that which brags about one's own personal abilities, merits, or distinctives (see, for example, the discussion in

For Thought and Discussion: How does 1:13 ("For we do not write . . .") support Paul's contention in 1:12 that he has always been sincere with the Corinthians?

For Further Study: Compare 2 Corinthians 2:10-11 with Matthew 6:14-15, Ephesians 4:26-27, and 1 Peter 3:7. What do they say about the correlation between sound personal relationships and our spiritual welfare?

2 Corinthians 10–13, as well as Philippians 3:2-11, where Paul uses the phrase "put confidence in the flesh" in much the same way as he does "boast" in 2 Corinthians 10–13).

___

1. Read 1:12-14. To what sort of accusation by his opponents at Corinth is Paul most likely replying here?

_____

_____

_____

_____

_____

___

Macedonia (1:16). The Roman province that corresponds to the northern portion of modern-day Greece. Macedonia was thus north of Corinth, which was the principal city of the province of Achaia (southern Greece).

2. What change did Paul make in his travel plans (see 1:15-16)? How did his opponents at Corinth use this against him (see 1:17)?

_____

_____

_____

_____

___

Anointed (1:21). From the Greek verb *chrio*, "to anoint." In the Old Testament, prophets (see 1 Kings 19:16), priests (see Exodus 28:41), and kings (see 1 Samuel 10:1) were anointed with oil, as a sign that the Spirit of God had called and specially equipped them for service. The Jews expected that one day such an "Anointed One" (Hebrew *Meshiach*, "Messiah"; Greek *Christos*, "Christ") would come to save

His people by fulfilling these three ministries of prophet, priest, and king. Here Paul does a play on words, using "Christ" and "anointed" (*chrisas*) in the same sentence.

Set his seal (1:22). An allusion to the act of stamping a document with one's personal seal imprinted in hot wax. This seal, often the top part of a signet ring, could be used as a pledge of fulfilling one's contractual obligations, such as full payment of a debt. Compare with Ephesians 4:30.

A deposit, guaranteeing what is to come (1:22). This phrase in the NIV translates one Greek word, which corresponds roughly to our modern "down payment," that is, a portion given as a guarantee that the entire payment will be made at a later date.

3. Paraphrase Paul's response to those who would accuse him of vacillation (see 1:18-22). Why do you think Paul's reply talks so much about the work of Christ?

_____

_____

_____

_____

_____

4. Paul changed his plans because of changing circumstances, yet consistently saw himself as having one purpose within the will of God (see 1:18-22). What was Paul's one purpose, or main objective, in relation to the church at Corinth?

_____

_____

_____

_____

_____

5. Have you ever had to change plans in order to accomplish your main objective? If so, write about it briefly.

_____

_____

_____

_____

_____

Why Paul changed his plans (1:23–2:4)

Another painful visit (2:1). Paul had already made one "painful visit" to Corinth. We do not know when this occurred. It certainly cannot have been his first visit to Corinth, when he founded the church there. Thus he must have made a second visit, probably between the writings of 1 and 2 Corinthians.

I wrote as I did . . . out of great distress (2:3-4). Until recently, most people saw this as a reference to 1 Corinthians. But while that letter does contain some points of reprimand, its tone can hardly be called one of "distress and anguish of heart" (2:4). It is therefore much more likely that Paul is referring to a letter written after 1 Corinthians but before 2 Corinthians, sometime after the "painful visit." This unknown letter is often called the "tearful letter."

6. Why did Paul write the "tearful letter" instead of visiting Corinth personally a third time after his second, "painful" visit (see 2:2-4)?

_____

_____

_____

_____

7. What do Paul's actions of 1:23–2:4 tell us about his character and his concern for the Corinthians?

_____

_____

_____

_____

_____

Discipline and forgiveness (2:5-11)

If anyone has caused grief (2:5). Someone had caused Paul great grief, probably by willfully challenging Paul's authority during his "painful visit."

Another possibility is that the one who caused Paul grief did so by refusing to repent of some ongoing sin in which he was already involved even before the apostle arrived. Some scholars, for example, see here a reference to the incestuous man of whom Paul speaks in 1 Corinthians 5:1-5. But if this is the case, why does Paul emphasize that he himself has personally forgiven the disobedient one (see 2:10)? Such personal forgiveness would make more sense if the sinful behavior were directed toward Paul himself, rather than toward someone else.

In either event, this man's sin evidently occasioned the "tearful letter" to which Paul refers in 2:4 (see also 2:9).

8. How did the Corinthians finally respond to the man whose misconduct had caused Paul such grief (see 2:6)?

_____

_____

_____

For Thought and Discussion: In 2:5-7 Paul speaks of church discipline. Have you ever seen such discipline exercised by the church? If so, what was the result?

Optional Application: Have you grieved anyone in the past week or so? If so, ask God to give you the wisdom and courage to undo the grief. Then take action to be reconciled, trusting that God can re-establish the broken relationship.

9. a. What effect did the Corinthians' response to this man's sin have on the man?

_____

_____

_____

_____

b. How, therefore, did Paul want the Corinthians to respond (see 2:6-8)?

_____

_____

_____

_____

10. According to Paul, why is it so important that the Corinthians follow Paul's example (see 2:10) and forgive this man (see 2:11)?

_____

_____

_____

_____

On to Macedonia (2:12-13)

Troas (2:12). The westernmost port city of the ancient province of Asia (modern Turkey), north of Ephesus and east of Macedonia (see map on page 9). Paul had been here at least once previously, when he first met Luke (see Acts 16:11; note the change to "we" in the travel narrative).

Titus (2:13). Paul had known Titus even before the apostle first visited Corinth (see, for example, Galatians 2:1-3). Paul evidently wanted to find Titus, who had been a coworker at Corinth, in order to find out how the Corinthians had responded to the "tearful letter."

11. Read 2:12-13, then reread carefully 1:23–2:4. Why was Paul so willing to leave Troas, despite an open door for ministry, in order to attempt to find Titus in Macedonia?

_____

_____

_____

_____

12. a. How do Paul's comments in 1:23–2:13 show his pastoral concern?

_____

_____

_____

b. What qualities do you see that are essential to a good pastoral ministry in the local church?

_____

_____

_____

For the group

Warm-up. A simple question that deals generally with the topic of the study but focuses on people's experience can help the group shift from the day's affairs to Bible study. A possible warm-up for this lesson: "How do you feel when someone postpones or cancels a social engagement to which you were looking forward?" Have everyone respond briefly; this will get them talking. Then, as the lesson proceeds, you may tie this in with how some of the Corinthians felt about Paul's change of plans (see 1:12-22).

Read aloud. Even when the group has studied the passage ahead of time, most people will be glad to have their memories refreshed. So read through all of 1:12–2:13 before beginning to discuss.

Summarize. A quick summary at the outset helps to set a context for the rest of the discussion. Briefly, what is 1:12–2:13 about? Do not try the sort of in-depth summary which normally comes at the end of a discussion, but do give the group a chance to observe the forest before you start analyzing trees.

Paul's singleness of purpose. Encourage group members to tie in Paul's concerns in 1:12-22 with his overall concern to establish his apostolic authority (see introduction). In addition, be sure to call attention to how Paul supports his singleness of purpose (i.e., the fact that he is not a fickle "yes-no" sort of person) with a theological explanation about Jesus Christ. Why all this theology in the middle of a personal conflict?

Paul's change of plans. At this point you might zero in on the "warm-up" question mentioned on page 31. Emphasize how changing situations may call for a change in plans in order to remain true to one's overall purpose or goal. How did Paul do this?

Discipline and forgiveness. As you answer the questions in this section, ask group members to reflect on the purpose of discipline. What is the difference, for example, between discipline and punishment?

On to Macedonia. Call attention to the fact that at the end of this section Paul breaks off the narrative account of his missionary travels, which he does not resume until 7:5. (Note that the word *Macedonia* occurs both in 2:13 and 7:5-6, as does Paul's mention of Titus.)

Summarize. Summarize the situation Paul found himself in as a result of the problems at Corinth and his response to them (the "tearful letter").

Wrap-up. Point out that lesson 3 begins a major digression in which Paul spells out the nature and purpose of his apostolic ministry. Encourage group members to prepare for next week by jotting down the ideas in 2:14–3:6 which most impress them.

Worship. Reread 1:18-22. Thank God that despite circumstances which seem contrary to His will for our lives, He always fulfills His promises to us in Jesus Christ.

Lesson Three

2 CORINTHIANS 2:14-3:6

"Who Is Equal to Such a Task?"

Second Corinthians 2:14 begins what many scholars label as "Paul's major digression." The apostle
begins with a great sigh of relief: "But thanks be
to God." The reader would naturally expect Paul
to continue his account of how he did finally ren-
dezvous with Titus in Macedonia, and how Titus
brought him the good news that the Corinthian
Christians had heeded the warnings of Paul's "tearful letter." This good news provided the immediate
occasion for Paul's exclamation of relief in 2:14.

Yet Paul departs from his narrative at this point
and does not pick it up again until 7:5. He instead
begins rejoicing, not merely in the Corinthians'
obedience to his gospel ministry, but also in the
all-surpassing greatness of that ministry itself. This
ministry so surpasses anything previously revealed
by God that human competence alone cannot fulfill
its demands. Only the power of God can do that
(see 2:16; 3:5).

Still, some at Corinth were trying to usurp Paul's
ministry, much to the apostle's distress. He has
already dealt by means of the "tearful letter" with one
who challenged his authority (see 2:5-7). Now he must
challenge others who would question his credentials
as an apostle (see 2:17–3:1). In so doing, his ultimate
appeal is not to himself, but to the gospel of Christ.

Triumph of the gospel (2:14-17)

*Leads us as captives in Christ's triumphal
procession* (2:14). Paul likens the advance of

33

For Further Study: Compare 2 Corinthians 2:14 with Colossians 2:13-15. Whom did Christ conquer, according to Paul? How did Christ do this?

For Thought and Discussion: Discuss 2 Corinthians 2:15-16 in light of Jesus' statements in Matthew 10:34-35.

the gospel to a Roman *triumphus,* or triumphal march, in which the victorious general leads his soldiers in public procession through the streets of Rome, with the prisoners of war following and exposed to public ridicule.[1]

Aroma (2:14-15). Paul continues the imagery of the triumphal march by alluding to sacrifices that were offered to Jupiter when the procession reached his temple, as well as to the incense that was burned in the streets.[2]

1. Paul thanks God, not for reuniting him with Titus or for the Corinthians' obedience to his apostolic authority, but for the spread of the gospel itself (see 2:14). What does this tell you about Paul's priorities in life?

   _____

   _____

   _____

2. a. Write down your own paraphrase of 2:14-16, identifying those who are leading in the procession and those who are watching it.

   _____

   _____

   _____

   _____

   b. Explain how the gospel ("good news") can become such bad news to some who hear it.

   _____

   _____

   _____

   _____

3. Rewrite Paul's rhetorical question in 2:16 as a simple statement.

_____

_____

_____

_____

_____

Study Skill—Rhetorical Questions
A rhetorical question is not really a question at all, but rather a statement put in the form of a question in order to have greater emotional impact. For example, the statement "I find that hard to believe" carries much more force when rephrased as "Are you kidding me?"

Rhetorical questions are also common in debate, often in order to force one's opponent to affirm or deny a point. Paul was particularly fond of such rhetorical questions (see Romans 6:1,15; 7:7,13), and he often wrote as though he were debating an adversary.

Negative rhetorical questions such as 1 Corinthians 9:1 ("Am I not free? Am I not an apostle?") require a positive response, and can thus be rewritten as positive declarative statements ("I *am* free; I *am* an apostle") in order to make their meaning clear. Rhetorical questions with no negative element (2 Corinthians 2:16, "Who is equal to such a task?") often require a negative response, and should then be expressed as negative statements. The context of the rhetorical question ultimately determines how it should be restated.

---

4. In 2:17, the NIV translation "so many" might be better expressed by "the majority." Is "the majority" to which Paul refers the majority of teachers at Corinth or the majority of Corinthian Christians in general? Explain your answer.

_____

_____

For Thought and Discussion: Do you think Paul means he is like one of the victorious soldiers in God's triumphal march (see 2:14), or is he like one of the prisoners on display? Why do you say that?

Optional Application: Can people sense the aroma of Christ when they are around you? What would make them more able to sense Christ?

For Thought and Discussion: Reread 3:1-3. Talk about how Christians should go about demonstrating the genuineness of their faith in Christ— and how they should not go about doing this.

_____

_____

_____

Letters of the heart (3:1-3)

Letters of recommendation (3:1). What we would today call "letters of reference." The practice was as widespread in Paul's day as in ours. Paul insisted he did not need any such letters, but did not object to the practice _per se_ (see, for example, Romans 16:1-2, Paul's brief letter of recommendation for Phoebe set within the larger epistle).

Tablets of stone (3:3). Almost certainly a reference to the tablets upon which the Law of Moses was written (see Exodus 24:12), as well as an allusion to God's promise to restore and regenerate the exiled nation of Israel (see Ezekiel 11:19; 36:26).

5. What are the two charges that Paul's opponents at Corinth brought against him in order to undermine his authority (see 3:1)?

_____

_____

_____

_____

6. In your own words, write Paul's response to his opponents' objections to his authority (see 3:2-3). Be sure to make clear the force of his argument.

_____

_____

_____

_____

_____

7. Read 3:3. One would expect Paul to follow the phrase "Written not with ink but with the Spirit . . ." with something like "[written] not on paper . . ." Why does he shift the metaphor and refer to "tablets of stone" (which are not a very good writing surface for ink)?

_____

_____

_____

A life-giving ministry (3:4-6)

Competent (3:5). The same word translated "equal" in 2:16 by the NIV.

New covenant (3:6). See Jeremiah 31:31–33, the first use of the term "new covenant" in the Bible. See also Ezekiel 11:19 and 36:26, which refer to the same promise.

In the Bible, a covenant is an agreement in which one party promises to do certain things for another party provided that second party meets certain conditions. The "old covenant" was God's promise to be Israel's God and to bless Israel if she remained faithful to God by trusting His promises and obeying His commands. The "new covenant" carries the same conditions, but is made not with a particular nation, but rather with individuals called out from every nation (see, for example, Acts 10:34-35).

Letter (3:6). Greek meaning literally "a letter [of the alphabet]," as opposed to the "letters" of 3:1, which are written documents (Greek *epistole*, "epistle"). The letter to which Paul refers to here is the written code inscribed on the tablets of stone at Sinai.

In Paul's thought, the written Law of God is "holy, righteous and good" (Romans 7:12). The Law "kills," not because it is evil but because sinful human nature cannot withstand its righteous judgments (much as darkness cannot survive once a lamp is lit in a dark room). Furthermore, the law becomes an occasion not

37

for salvation, but for further sinful acts, because our "sinful passions" are "aroused by the law" (Romans 7:5). That is to say, when the Law urges us to follow God, our sinful nature rebels.

According to Paul, the fundamental rebellion of Israel was that she misconstrued the Law, which urged people to trust God's promises in order to be saved. Instead, Israel turned God's commands into a sort of merit-badge system, so that people could claim salvation by reliance upon their own efforts ("works") rather than reliance upon God's promises and power ("faith"). See Romans 9:30-32, where Paul makes it clear that Israel's sin was that she pursued the Law "as if it were by works": that is, contrary to its original intent, which was to teach what Paul calls "the obedience that comes from faith" (Romans 1:5).

For Paul, then, the problem with the "letter" of the Law is that it has no power in itself to turn people from sin. Only when God, through the gift of His Spirit, gives a person a "new heart" (Ezekiel 36:26) does the Law become an "aroma that brings life" rather than an "aroma that brings death" (2 Corinthians 2:16). Otherwise, sinful people will misconstrue the Law (whether inadvertently or deliberately) and try to turn it into a means of earning salvation through one's own efforts.

In the gospel accounts Jesus points to the Pharisees as a prime example of this. They kept the "letter" of the Law, but missed its "spirit" entirely (see, for example, Matthew 23:23). Jesus, on the other hand, came not to abolish the Law, but to fulfill it (see Matthew 5:17).

Thus, Paul is in agreement with Jesus. Both sought to set aside not the Law itself but rather legalistic interpretations which had made the Law into a tool of self-justification by appealing to its words ("letter") while missing its true meaning.

---

8. a. In what two things does Paul refuse to place his confidence (see 3:1,5)?

_____

_____

b. What, then, is the basis of his confidence in the ministry he has undertaken (see 3:4-5)?

_____

_____

_____

_____

9. Reread 3:1-5. What sorts of qualifications are important for a minister of the gospel, and which are not? (Feel free to add to what Paul says.)

important	not important

10. Compare 3:6 with Jeremiah 31:33. What is "new" about the new covenant, according to Jeremiah and Paul?

_____

_____

_____

_____

_____

For Thought and Discussion: Does 3:6 mean that (a) Christians are no longer responsible for obeying the Law, or (b) Christians, unlike most of those who were under the old covenant, have been given the power to obey the Law? Explain your answer.

Optional Application: How confident (see 3:4) do you feel before God? If you were to stand before God today and He asked you, "Why should I allow you into My heaven?" what would you say? Examine your answer in light of Paul's teaching in 3:4-6.

Optional Application: Examine your own spiritual life. Are there any ways in which you are living by the "letter" and not by the "Spirit"? Ask God to give you wisdom to discern the difference, and power to walk in the Spirit.

11. State briefly in your own words why it is that "the letter kills" (3:6).

_____

_____

_____

_____

_____

12. Read 3:6 in light of Deuteronomy 29:4 and Ezekiel 36:26. What is it that "the Spirit" can provide under the new covenant that "the letter" of the Mosaic covenant could not?

_____

_____

_____

_____

_____

13. How would you explain to someone what it means to be a member of the "new covenant" (a Christian)?

_____

_____

_____

_____

Your response

14. What statement in 2:14–3:6 seems most personally significant to you?

_____

_____

_____

_____

_____

15. How would you like to respond to this
statement?

_____

_____

_____

_____

16. List any questions you have about 2:14–3:6.

_____

_____

_____

_____

_____

For the group

Warm-up. You may wish to ask if anyone has any
further reflection on lesson 2. For a warm-up to lesson 3, you might try this: "Think of someone you
know who exudes an aroma of Christ when you are
around him or her. What quality does that person
have that reminds you of Christ?"

Read aloud and summarize. Before going into the
study questions for lesson 3, point out the three
main divisions of the lesson (2:14-17; 3:1-3; 3:4-6)
and restate Paul's main point in each.

Triumph of the gospel. Group members may be
somewhat taken aback by Paul's reference to the
gospel ministry as carrying an "aroma that brings
death" (2:16) for some. Allow participants to express
their feelings about this candidly, and work hard as

a group to understand how it is that the gospel can become an occasion of spiritual death for some.

Letters of the heart. Ask group members how important letters of reference are in today's business and professional world. Why does Paul feel no need of such letters?

A life-giving ministry. Point out that Paul answers his own rhetorical question of 2:16 in 3:4. And be sure that group members understand what Paul means by "the letter kills, but the Spirit gives life" (3:6), since that verse leads directly into next week's lesson.

Summarize. Recap what you've learned about the methods and message of Paul's opponents, as well as Paul's own message.

Wrap-up. Advise people that the text to be covered in lesson 4 (3:7–4:6), while not overly long, is extremely difficult to understand. You may find it helpful to spend two sessions on this upcoming lesson.

Worship. Praise God for giving His Spirit to enable believers to live out the Christian life, as opposed to leaving us to our own strength.

1. Murray J. Harris, *2 Corinthians*, The Expositor's Bible Commentary, vol. 10, ed. Frank E. Gaebelein (Grand Rapids, MI: Zondervan, 1976), 331–332.
2. Harris, 332.

Lesson Four

2 CORINTHIANS 3:7-4:6

The Glory of the New Covenant

In this section, one of the most difficult in all of Paul's writings, the apostle goes on to elaborate on his statement of 3:6, "The letter kills, but the Spirit gives life." Specifically, he contrasts the results of the old covenant ministry as instituted by Moses with the results of the new covenant ministry. The contrast is threefold: (1) The Mosaic ministry resulted, for the most part, in death for its hearers; the ministry of the Spirit brings life; (2) the Mosaic ministry was temporary; the ministry of the Spirit is everlasting; (3) the Mosaic ministry lacked the power to enlighten the hearts of its hearers; the ministry of the Spirit brings that light necessary for obedience to God.

The new covenant brings life, not death (3:7-11)

By speaking of "covenant," Paul indicates that at least some of his opponents in Corinth were probably "Judaizers" who were teaching the Gentile Corinthians that they must strictly follow the Law of Moses in order to be saved. In other words, more than Paul's apostolic authority was at issue in Corinth; the very essence of the gospel was at stake. For this reason Paul chooses to elaborate not on his own qualifications, but on the gospel message.

Ministry that brought death (3:7). Literally, "ministry of death." The NIV correctly interprets

For Further Study:
Read the account of Moses and the veil in Exodus 34:29-35. Make a list of similarities and differences between this text and Paul's account of the same episode in 2 Corinthians 3:12-18.

For Further Study:
Read Romans 7:7-25. Jot down what Paul says about the Law, and try to harmonize this with 2 Corinthians 3:7–4:6.

Paul's meaning here: the old covenant resulted in death for most who heard it. Paul was elaborating on teaching he had already shared with the Corinthians (see 1 Corinthians 10:1-5). The apparent paradox that the Law, although good in and of itself, ended up as a death sentence for so many, is explained by Paul in Romans 7:5-24 (see especially 7:10). It is important to distinguish between the old covenant Law itself (which is good) and the ministry of the old covenant, which resulted in death, not because the Law was evil, but because sinful people refused to obey it.

Its glory, transitory though it was (3:7). A reference to the glorious radiance of Moses' face as described in Exodus 34:29-35. When Moses brought the Ten Commandments down from Mount Sinai, "his face was radiant because he had spoken with the LORD" (34:29). The Israelites were afraid to come near Moses because of this radiance. Moses nevertheless called them to him and told them what God had commanded. After doing so, however, he placed a veil over his face, which shielded at least some of the radiance from his fellow Israelites.

In addition, whenever Moses would enter the tabernacle and speak with the Lord, he would remove the veil. And after this, "when he came out and told the Israelites what he had been commanded, they saw that his face was radiant. Then Moses would put the veil back over his face until he went in to speak with the LORD" (34:34-35).

Paul's use of this passage is extremely difficult to interpret, because he draws a significance from it which goes beyond the original meaning of the Old Testament writer. Perhaps from the fact that Moses' face was radiant every time he came out of the tabernacle, Paul describes this radiance as "transitory" or fading. To use a modern analogy, Moses needed to "recharge his batteries" from time to time by entering the tabernacle, lest the radiance of his face (which symbolized the glory of God) fade away. Yet even at that, the people of Israel did not wish to gaze steadily upon Moses' radiant face.

1. Second Corinthians 3:7-8 is a classic example of an argument from the lesser to the greater: "If X is true, then Y is much more true." According to this passage, why is the ministry of the Spirit (Paul's ministry) much more glorious than the ministry of the Law (Moses' ministry)? Explain in your own words.

_____

_____

_____

_____

_____

_____

2. a. What is transitory in 3:7?

_____

_____

b. What is transitory in 3:11?

_____

_____

c. How are they related?

_____

_____

_____

3. In 3:11, what is the difference between the old covenant and the new covenant?

_____

_____

_____

_____

For Further Study: Read Jeremiah 31:31-33. According to God, what is the difference between the old and new covenants? See also Ezekiel 11:19; 18:31; 36:26-38; 37:14.

For Thought and Discussion: In Paul's mind, what is the difference between the Law of Moses on the one hand, and the "letter" on the other?

For Thought and Discussion: What was there about the old covenant that caused Paul to characterize it as a "ministry that brought death" (3:7)?

The new covenant unveils an everlasting glory (3:12-18)

4. To what do the words "such a hope" (3:12) refer? (Remember that the word *therefore* refers to what immediately precedes.)

_____

_____

_____

_____

_____

5. Paraphrase 3:12, making clear just what it is that makes Paul act so boldly.

_____

_____

_____

_____

_____

_____

The end of what was passing away (3:13). Literally, "unto the end of that which was fading away." Here, as in verse 11, "what was passing away" is neuter in gender. It therefore does not refer to "the glory" or radiance of Moses' face (as it does in verse 9), since the word *glory* is feminine. Rather, "what was passing away" was the old covenant itself, of which the radiance of Moses' face was a symbol. We might therefore paraphrase 3:13 as follows: "Moses put a veil over his face in order to keep the people of Israel from seeing that the [radiance of the] old covenant would keep passing away until it eventually came to an end." Just why Moses would want to *veil* the temporary nature of the old covenant from the Israelites is uncertain. What is important for Paul is that Moses could not act as boldly as he (Paul), since the old covenant was not as glorious a covenant as the new covenant.

6. If "the same veil" in 3:14 refers to the veil of 3:13, what is being hidden from the Israelites that has made their minds "dull" to the true nature of the old covenant?

_____

_____

_____

_____

7. According to Paul, how can this dullness be overcome (see 3:14)?

_____

_____

_____

_____

8. How does the glory of the new covenant differ from that of the old covenant (see 3:18)?

_____

_____

_____

_____

The new covenant enlightens our hearts (4:1-6)

9. According to 4:2, what may have been some of the accusations made by Paul's opponents at Corinth?

_____

_____

For Thought and Discussion: Discuss how Paul's contrast between the old and new covenants would strengthen his apostolic authority over opponents who were "Judaizers."

For Thought and Discussion: What does it mean to reflect the Lord's glory, practically speaking?

Optional Application: Thank God this week that He gives to those who believe in Christ not only the knowledge of the truth, but the power to obey it.

Optional Application: How should 4:4 affect the way we view unbelievers and the way we go about evangelism?

_____

_____

_____

10. Why, according to Paul, did his opponents not understand his ministry (see 4:3-4)?

_____

_____

_____

_____

_____

11. a. What does Paul imply that his opponents were doing, and that he was not doing (see 4:5)?

_____

_____

_____

_____

_____

b. How was this behavior of Paul's opponents related to their spiritual blindness spoken of in 4:3-4?

_____

_____

_____

_____

_____

12. Review 4:1-6. How can we avoid having the gospel veiled in our own lives?

For Thought and Discussion: What keeps us from thinking of the gospel as glorious?

_____

_____

_____

_____

_____

_____

_____

13. In the chart below, write down the threefold contrast between the two covenants Paul makes in 3:7–4:6.

old covenant	new covenant
1.	1.
2.	2.
3.	3.

Optional Application: Pray that God will transform one specific area of your life into greater conformity to Christ (see 3:18).

Optional Application: Are you aware of reflecting the Lord's glory in your daily life? What difference would it make if you thought about this as you went through your day?

Your response

14. Write down one new truth you have learned from this lesson.

_____

_____

_____

_____

15. How is this truth relevant to your life?

_____

_____

_____

_____

16. List any questions you have about this challenging passage.

_____

_____

_____

_____

For the group

Warm-up. Ask everyone what picture they get in their minds when they think of glory. When everyone has responded, explain that in Hebrew, glory came from a word that meant "weight." The word was also used to describe the glowing cloud that led Israel through the wilderness. This idea of glowing bright light comes through in the image of Moses' radiant face. Glory is weighty and substantive, and it is radiant light. How do these images help you envision what Paul is getting at in this passage?

Read aloud and summarize. Note the three contrasts Paul makes between the old covenant and the new covenant.

Life, not death. Make sure group members understand what it was about the old covenant ministry that made it so much less glorious than the new covenant. Specifically, the difference lay not in what the old covenant demanded (which is the same as the new covenant: the Law of God; see Jeremiah 31:31-34), but rather in what the old covenant did not possess: the promise of the indwelling Spirit.

An everlasting glory unveiled. Pose the question, "Why was the old covenant temporary?" As you discuss this, be sure to center on the relationship between Old Testament promises and their fulfillment in Christ.

Enlightened hearts. Have group members share what the phrase "the glory of Christ" means in their personal experience.

Wrap-up.

Worship. Thank God that He would share His own glory—the very glory of Christ—with the undeserving, people such as us.

2 CORINTHIANS 4:7–5:10

Priceless Treasure in Cracked Pots

Paul's life as a minister of the gospel was not easy. He suffered great hardships, some to which he has already alluded in this letter (see 1:8-11) and others he mentions later on (see 6:4-10; 11:23-29). His opponents at Corinth evidently used Paul's sufferings as an argument that he was not experiencing the sort of "victorious Christian life" that ought to earmark a true apostle. In short, they were portraying Paul as a sort of spiritual wimp.

As he defends his ministry in this section, Paul does not try to deny this. Rather, he contends that his sufferings are not marks of God's disapproval, but are instead one of God's ways of refusing to share His glory with anyone else. For the meaning of the gospel is seen most clearly when God's power to deliver the helpless is made manifest.

Through death to life (4:7-15)

Jars of clay (4:7). Earthenware vessels used for carrying water. Such pottery was easily broken and thus of little value in and of itself, since it could easily be replaced.

1. In 4:7, "this treasure" and "this all-surpassing power" refer to something in the previous paragraph. To what do these two parallel phrases refer?

For Thought and Discussion: Discuss as a group any experiences you may have had in which God's power became even more evident to others because of your own weakness.

_____

_____

_____

2. In 4:8-9 Paul lists four ways in which his own weakness gives opportunity for God to display His power. Write out these four contrasts, using your own words to make Paul's meaning clear.

_____

_____

_____

_____

_____

_____

3. Paul's language in 4:8-9 has been likened to a description of military combat. What does this tell us about his view of the nature of the gospel ministry?

_____

_____

_____

_____

4. Why do you think Paul refers to his sufferings as "the death of Jesus" (4:10)?

_____

_____

_____

_____

5. In 4:11, do you think Paul is saying that Jesus' life is being revealed in his body *while* he suffers, or that Jesus' life will be revealed in his body *after* Paul has suffered, died, and been resurrected? Explain your view.

_____

_____

_____

_____

_____

6. a. What motivates Paul to preach the gospel in spite of hardships (see 4:13-14)?

_____

_____

_____

_____

b. What role does this same hope play in your own life?

_____

_____

_____

_____

Optional Application: In Paul's experience, the "death of Jesus" always had to precede the "life of Jesus" (4:10). How might you apply this to your own walk with the Lord?

For Further Study: Compare 2 Corinthians 4:13 with Psalm 116:10. What do Paul and the psalmist whom he quotes have in common? How did God respond to each of them?

We live by faith, not by sight

(4:16–5:10)

Earthly tent (5:1). The metaphor of "tent" for a temporary dwelling would come naturally to Paul, who by trade was a tentmaker (see Acts 18:3). He may also be alluding to the Old

For Thought and Discussion:
a. In light of 5:1, how do you think Paul would react to our modern emphasis on youthful appearance and physical fitness if he were alive today?

b. Compare 3:18 and 5:1. What perspective do these verses give on the pursuit of physical beauty?

For Thought and Discussion: What difference, if any, does it make to you that the Christian hope is resurrection of the body, and not merely immortality of the soul?

Optional Application: Choose one of the "unseen realities" referred to in 4:17 and in question 7, and apply it to your prayer life this week.

Testament tabernacle, a large tent which served as a portable and temporary house for the Lord until nomadic Israel settled into the more sedentary lifestyle of a kingdom and built a temple.

A building from God, an eternal house in heaven (5:1). The words *building* and *house* denote permanent structures, as opposed to a temporary dwelling such as a tent. At the same time, however, they are physical structures like a tent.

In 1 Corinthians 15 we see that not all of the Corinthians shared Paul's view that Christians would be resurrected in physical bodies. They believed instead that any *resurrection* was purely spiritual in nature, consisting of spiritual enlightenment which came from knowing the risen Christ. This sort of mentality was influenced by Greek gnostic philosophy, which viewed the body as evil and saw salvation as liberation from the body and immortality of the soul, to be accomplished through knowledge of secret, divine wisdom (hence "gnostics," from the Greek word meaning "knowledge"). Such "Christian" gnostics rejected any notion of a bodily resurrection; hence, Paul found it necessary to reject their teachings vigorously (see 1 Corinthians 15:12-55). He may have had these same heretics in mind as he wrote 2 Corinthians 5:1-10.

7. Read 4:16-18. List two or three elements of the Christian faith which you cannot see, but which are central to your faith. Why are these important to you?

_____

_____

_____

_____

_____

_____

_____

8. If "tent" (5:1) refers indirectly to the tabernacle of the old covenant, how does Paul's discussion here coincide with his remarks in 3:7-11, which contrast the old and new covenants?

_____

_____

_____

_____

_____

9. According to Paul, why did God create us (see 5:4-5)?

_____

_____

_____

_____

_____

10. Paul says that Christians "live by faith, not by sight" (5:7). What does Paul mean in this context by this often-quoted expression?

_____

_____

_____

_____

_____

11. In 5:8-10, what two future realities motivate Paul to please the Lord in all he says and does?

_____

_____

_____

_____

_____

Optional Application: What does it mean to you personally to "live by faith, not by sight" (5:7)?

For Further Study: Compare 2 Corinthians 5:10 with 1 Corinthians 3:10-15 and 4:3-5. Write down everything Paul says about what will happen when Christians appear before the judgment seat of Christ.

Optional Application: In light of Paul's teaching on the "judgment seat of Christ" (5:10), ask God to show you one area of your life that you would like to bring into closer obedience to Him. If you feel comfortable doing so, share this with the group and ask them to pray for you.

12. In your own words, tell why Paul can feel totally confident in the face of ill health and death (see 5:1-10).

_____

_____

_____

_____

_____

Your response

13. What truth in this passage seems personally significant to you today?

_____

_____

_____

_____

_____

14. How will you respond?

_____

_____

_____

_____

_____

15. List any questions you have about 4:7–5:10.

_____

_____

_____

_____

For the group

Warm-up. In a sentence or two, share one source of stress in your life right now.

Read aloud and summarize.

Through death to life. As you study the contrast between Christ's strength ("treasure") and the Christian's weakness ("jars of clay"), be sure to distinguish between the weaknesses of infirmity and affliction on the one hand, and moral transgression on the other. Discuss why Christ can be glorified in the first type of weakness, but not in the second.

"We live by faith, not by sight." This phrase (5:7) can be used to mean a number of things—not all of them consistent with what Paul had in mind! For example, Paul makes it clear throughout his writings that Christian faith is based not on mere ideas, but on events seen by eyewitnesses, including himself, at a specific point in history (see 1 Corinthians 15:3-8). In this sense, Christian faith involves "sight."

What is it, then, that Paul does not see, but that motivates him to continue obeying God ("live by faith")? Have group members share their responses to question 10; what does this phrase mean in the context of 5:5-9?

Wrap-up. The contrast between Christ's glory (see 3:7–4:6) and our weakness (see 4:7–5:10) makes it necessary to live by faith in God's promise that we shall one day experience total deliverance from affliction. Without this promise of future freedom from earthly trials, we may be tempted to conclude that because our lives right now do not share in the heavenly glory of Christ, we may not be Christians.

Worship. Thank God that the gift of His Holy Spirit is but a "deposit, guaranteeing what is to come" (5:5). We have an eternal glory to look forward to!

Lesson Six

2 CORINTHIANS 5:11-6:2

The Ministry of Reconciliation

Thus far Paul has emphasized the glorious power of the new covenant, a power that gives the apostle hope even in the fear of death. Now he moves on and details more specifically what the good news of the new covenant is all about: God has reconciled sinful people to Himself through the person and work of Jesus Christ. This is the core of the gospel.

Motivation for ministry (5:11-15)

1. To what do the words "since, then" (5:11; Greek "therefore") refer?

   _____

   _____

   _____

   _____

2. Referring to your answer to question 1, what does Paul mean in this context by the expression "fear the Lord" (5:11)?

   _____

   _____

   _____

   _____

   _____

3. Why was Paul so concerned to justify his apostolic ministry to the Corinthian Christians (see 5:12)?

_____

_____

_____

_____

_____

_____

4. According to Paul, how were his opponents building themselves up at Paul's expense (see 5:12)? Contrast their behavior with Paul's.

_____

_____

_____

_____

_____

If we are "out of our mind" (5:13). No doubt a charge leveled at Paul by his opponents in Corinth. Exactly what led them to do so remains unclear. Among the possible accusations are: (1) Paul's esoteric teachings, often difficult to understand or accept, led his detractors to label him as "out of his mind." (2) Paul is referring to his mystical experiences such as "tongues" and visions (see Acts 22:17-21). (3) Paul was often carried away with emotion. (4) Paul was preoccupied with self-commendation (see 3:1; 5:12). (5) In Jewish eyes, Paul's conversion was sheer lunacy.[1]

5. Do you think the word *all*, which occurs three times in 5:14-15, refers to all people in general or all people who believe in Christ? Why?

_____

_____

_____

_____

_____

For Thought and Discussion: How can a Christian be motivated both by the fear of the Lord (see 5:11) and Christ's love (see 5:14)?

6. Write out 5:15, substituting "I" and "me" where appropriate.

_____

_____

_____

_____

_____

7. What is one way in which you would like to "live for Christ" this week?

_____

_____

_____

_____

The message of reconciliation (5:16–6:2)

From a worldly point of view (5:16). Literally, "according to the flesh." In Paul's letters "flesh" is often used to denote a perspective opposed to the things of God—in other words, a worldly point of view (because Paul views the world as sinful). See Romans 8:1-17 for Paul's classic treatment of the contrast between the Spirit and the flesh.

For Further Study: Compare 2 Corinthians 5:17 with Romans 12:2, Ephesians 4:22-24, and Colossians 3:1-11. Write down what it means to you to be a "new creation" in Christ.

8. Paraphrase 2 Corinthians 5:15-17, making use of the clues from the word *therefore*.

_____

_____

_____

_____

_____

_____

_____

_____

_____

_____

Study Skill—Inferences

Words such as *since, then* (5:11), *so* (5:16), and *therefore* (5:17) are used to indicate inferences. That is, the sentence or paragraph which precedes such words serves as an argument or an evidence for what follows. The French philosopher Descartes' statement "I think, therefore I am" is a classic example of such an inference.

In following Paul's line of argumentation, it is important to pay close attention to such inferences. In each case, the reader should look at the statement preceding a word such as *therefore* in order to discover the basis for what Paul says after the *therefore*. For example, in the NIV, 2 Corinthians 5:16 begins with the word *so*. The reader should then look at the statement which precedes (5:15) to see if 5:16 is a reasonable inference from it.

In rare instances a "therefore" statement is supported by a statement which does not immediately precede it. In 5:17, "therefore" refers to 5:15. (In the Greek, "so" in verse 16 and "therefore" in verse 17 are the same word so it's clear they are parallel statements referring to verse 15).

9. Read 5:16-17. Contrast a worldly point of view ("the old") with a Christian point of view ("the new") about Jesus, the Bible, human nature, and the future.

Optional Application: As you pray this week, thank God specifically for sending Christ to die for your sins, and pray for wisdom and strength to live for Christ rather than for self (see 5:15).

	the old view	the new view
Jesus		
the Bible		
human nature		
the future		

For Thought and Discussion: Why was it necessary for Christ to die in order for us to be reconciled to God (see 5:21)? (You may wish to refer to Paul's lengthy discussions in Romans 3:21-31 and 5:12-21.)

For Further Study: Compare and contrast Paul's statements concerning Christ's sinlessness (see 5:21) with those of 1 Peter 2:22, 1 John 3:5, and Hebrews 4:15; 7:26.

10. Look up *reconcile* in a dictionary and write out a definition that fits Paul's usage of this word in 5:18-20.

_____

_____

_____

_____

_____

11. How was the Holy God able to accomplish reconciliation between Himself and sinful humanity (see 5:21)?

_____

_____

_____

_____

_____

We urge you (6:1). The verb translated "urge" here is derived from the same word Paul uses in 1:3-7 when speaking of the "comfort" of God. See the note on comfort from 1:3-7 on page 19.

12. In 5:20 and 6:1 Paul appears to be making evangelistic appeals to people who are already Christians (i.e., his Corinthian readers). How do these appeals relate to his overall concern that the Corinthians recognize and accept his apostolic authority?

_____

_____

_____

_____

_____

13. How does Paul indicate that this reconciliation is not confined to the future but is happening at the present time (see 6:1-2)?

_____

_____

_____

_____

_____

For Thought and Discussion: What does it mean to "receive God's grace in vain" (6:1)?

Your response

14. Write down one new truth you learned from this lesson about the death of Christ.

_____

_____

_____

_____

15. How will you apply this to your life?

_____

_____

_____

_____

_____

16. List any questions you have about 5:11–6:2.

_____

_____

_____

_____

For the group

Warm-up. Because at least five weeks have gone by since this study of 2 Corinthians began, you may wish to take inventory and find out what people have liked about the study thus far, and invite suggestions as to how the format might be improved. (Do not spend so long on this that you fail to get into this week's lesson.)

Read aloud and summarize.

Questions. Spend some time talking about motivation. What motivates Paul to act as he does on the Corinthians' behalf (see 5:15)? Discuss how group members can apply this to their relationships with others.

Second Corinthians 5:17-21 represents in summary form the heart of the gospel of Jesus Christ. Have group members discuss the meaning of the following terms (among others):

- New creature (see 5:17)
- The old versus the new (see 5:17)
- Reconciled/reconciliation (see 5:18)
- Sins (see 5:19)
- Sin (see 5:21)
- Righteousness of God (see 5:21)

Wrap-up. Have group members summarize briefly by answering the question "What is the gospel?"

Worship.

1. Murray J. Harris, *2 Corinthians*, The Expositor's Bible Commentary, vol. 10, ed. Frank E. Gaebelein (Grand Rapids, MI: Zondervan, 1976), 351.

2 CORINTHIANS 6:3-7:4

A Pastor's Plea to His Troubled Flock

After spelling out the heart of the gospel message and exhorting the Corinthians to embrace it (see 5:11–6:2), Paul again feels it necessary to defend the authenticity of his apostolic authority. He does so first by spelling out the hardships of apostolic service, then warning the Corinthians not to fraternize with those who would lead them astray.

The perils of Paul (6:3-10)

1. What relationship does Paul see between the credibility of the gospel message and the lifestyle of the gospel messengers (see 6:3)?

_____

_____

_____

_____

_____

_____

In 6:4-10 Paul records a litany of trials surrounding his ministry. When reading such passages, the temptation is to skim over them in order to gain a general impression of the whole section, without examining each element closely. Such an approach leaves us with the sense that Paul had to deal with many difficulties, but gives little insight as to the specific nature of these difficulties.

Beatings, imprisonments and riots (6:5). Some of Paul's trials were caused by other people hostile to his mission. Jews who thought he was teaching heresy repeatedly attacked him (see Acts 14:1-7; 17:5-9). Greeks who were making good livings from paganism, like the owners of a fortune-telling slave and the silversmiths who made souvenirs of an Ephesian goddess, became violent when Paul's presence threatened their livelihoods (see Acts 16:16-24; 19:23-41).

In hard work, sleepless nights and hunger (6:5). In twenty years of missionary journeys, Paul traveled about 1,500 miles on foot and another 1,300 or so by sea. Hiking across rugged Asia Minor was no small feat in the days before hiking boots, aluminum-frame backpacks, and freeze-dried food. There were inns every twenty-two miles on a Roman road, but twenty-two miles a day is a stiff pace in good weather, and impossible if the road was muddy or steep, so Paul probably spent many rainy or snowy nights huddled under a leather tent. Farmers avoided selling food to travelers, so hunger was another given. Even if Paul reached an inn by nightfall, he would have slept either outside with the animals by a dung fire, or inside with several other travelers and a small army of bedbugs.

---

2. What inward virtues and spiritual equipment enabled Paul to endure such conditions (see 6:6-7)?

_____

_____

_____

_____

_____

3. Which of these qualities would have been hardest for you to maintain through nights without dinner or sleep, or when people attacked you? Why would that be hard for you?

_____

_____

_____

_____

_____

_____

4. How was Paul able to maintain an attitude of "sincere love" and always practice "truthful speech" (6:6-7) amid constant persecution?

_____

_____

_____

_____

_____

5. What sorts of responses can we expect when we share the gospel with others (see 6:8-10)?

_____

_____

_____

_____

_____

6. In the chart, contrast the accusations Paul's opponents made against him with the reality Paul experienced as an ambassador for Christ (see 6:9-10).

For Thought and Discussion: Why was Paul willing to endure so much for the sake of those who might come to know Christ? How does one acquire that outlook on life?

Optional Application: Focus on one of the four virtues Paul mentions in 6:6 (purity, understanding, patience, kindness), and pray this week that God will teach you to apply this virtue in one significant relationship in your life.

For Further Study:
Second Corinthians
6:14 is often applied
to marriage, though
that is not Paul's
intent here. Compare
this text with his
discussion of "mixed
marriages" in
1 Corinthians 7:12-16.

**For Thought and
Discussion:** Second
Corinthians 6:14–7:1
has been called a
digression because
its relationship to
Paul's main line of
argument in 6:3–7:4 is
not apparent to some
scholars. Discuss how
you see this section
fitting into Paul's
exhortations to the
Corinthians found in
6:3–7:4.

accusations	reality

A plea for loyalty (6:11–7:4)

7. Paul felt the Corinthians were withholding their
full loyalty and affection from him (see 6:11-13).
What do you think caused them to do this?

_____

_____

_____

_____

Yoked together (6:14). See Deuteronomy 22:10,
where the Law of Moses prohibited the yoking
together of an ox and a donkey for plowing.
This was done for the benefit of the donkey,
who lacked the strength to work together with
the more powerful ox and whose health would
be damaged by working with the larger animal.

8. Who are the "unbelievers" to whom Paul refers
in 6:14? Do you think they are non-Christians
in general or Paul's opponents in Corinth who
claimed to be following God properly? Give
reasons for your answer, including any relevant passages from Paul's writings, such as
1 Corinthians 5:9-13 and 10:27.

_____

_____

_____

_____

_____

9. Why is it both wrong and dangerous for Christians to be "yoked together with unbelievers" (6:14)?

_____

_____

_____

_____

Belial (6:15). A Hebrew expression meaning "worthlessness," it was used in later Jewish literature to refer to the Devil. This seems to be Paul's usage here.

10. What do you think Paul means by urging Christians to "come out" and "be separate" from non-Christian influences (see 6:16-18)? Compare 1 Corinthians 5:9-13.

_____

_____

_____

_____

11. Compare 7:2-4 with 6:11-13. In what ways are these passages alike? How do they differ?

_____

_____

_____

For Thought and Discussion: How would it feel to be Paul, who endured so much for the sake of his converts and then was treated as the Corinthians treated him?

Optional Application: Do you know anyone whom you like, yet who frustrates you on occasion? (A friend? A child?) Paul knew a whole church like that! Pray that through this week's lesson God might teach you to deal wisely with such friends (or with yourself if you are such a friend).

_____

_____

12. Briefly summarize Paul's attitude toward
    the Corinthians, and their attitude toward
    Paul.

Paul's attitude	the Corinthians' attitude

Your response

13. What struck you as personally significant in
    6:3–7:4?

    _____

    _____

    _____

    _____

14. How should this affect the way you live your
    life?

    _____

    _____

    _____

    _____

15. List any questions you have about this passage.

_____

_____

_____

_____

_____

_____

For the group

Warm-up.

Read aloud.

Summarize. In this section (6:3–7:4), note Paul's simultaneous concern (see 6:13; 7:2) and confidence (see 7:3-4) with regard to the Corinthians. Point out that this lesson deals chiefly with Paul's concern; the next lesson, which covers 7:5-16, tells us why, despite these concerns, Paul also had reason to be confident.

Questions. Paul lists the hardships of his ministry, not to impress the Corinthians with his abilities, but to demonstrate his concern for them. For example, he specifically attributes his perseverance to the Holy Spirit and the power of God (see 6:6-7).

Spend time discussing Paul's list of 6:4-10. Notice in particular what he suffered through by persecution and calamity, what he endured by choice, and the personal qualities which he displayed through his hardships. Also, try to discern some of the criticisms his opponents were making of him. Then discuss what is different from what you have experienced, and what is similar. How does thinking about Paul's endurance make you feel?

The crucial section 6:14–7:1 has been applied to questions of marriage and business partnership (see 6:14), as well as whether or not to separate from an "impure" church (see 6:17-18). Be sure to center on what Paul is dealing with in this context! Having done that, you will be in a better position to apply Paul's message to your life without reading into the apostle's words ideas that were not there originally.

The problem of 6:1–7:1. Many modern translations, including the NIV, regard 6:14–7:1 as a minor digression between 6:13 and 7:2. The tone is markedly different from what precedes and follows, and the entire section could be lifted out without appearing to interrupt the flow of Paul's argument.

This study guide, however, views 6:11–7:4 as a unity. Make sure the group understands how this study guide connects 6:14–7:1 with what precedes and what follows: In 6:11-13 Paul's message is positive: "Open your hearts to me and my ministry." In 6:14–7:1 Paul states the negative side of this exhortation: "Do not become involved with the false teachers (unbelievers) in your midst." He then concludes by repeating his positive plea, "Open your hearts," adding to it expressions of confidence (see 7:2-4).

Some members of the study group, of course, may interpret the relationship between these verses differently. But it is important to come to terms with how the study guide views the text, so that if one wishes to adopt a different point of view, that decision will be an informed one.

Wrap-up. Call attention to the balance Paul tries to maintain between positive exhortation and strong negative warnings in 6:11–7:4.

Worship.

2 CORINTHIANS 7:5-16

Effects of Spiritual Discipline

Paul longed for the Corinthians to be as openly affectionate and candid with him as he was with them (see 6:13; 7:2). His relationship with them had not attained the depths of Christian love that he desired. Yet while the church at Corinth was far from perfect, nevertheless a significant measure of healing and reconciliation had already taken place between Paul and his wayward flock, even as he was exhorting them to greater loyalty and affection.

For this reason, the apostle now turns from exhortation to commendation, expressing his joy that the Corinthians have changed their attitude toward him and his ministry as a result of his "tearful letter." Specifically, he resumes the narrative that he interrupted at 2:13 in order to deal with some underlying theological issues.

Comfort in Macedonia (7:5-7)

Where did Paul last mention his journey to Macedonia and his desire to see Titus? Reread 2:12-13, then skip over everything Paul wrote between that section and 7:5 in order to get a sense of the continuity of the narrative.

1. Paul speaks of "conflicts on the outside" and "fears within" (7:5) during his visit to Macedonia. He even mentions being "downcast" (7:6). Does it surprise you that Paul wrestled with fear and low emotions? Why, or why not?

For Thought and Discussion: Compare 7:6-7 with 1:3-7, and discuss how the Corinthians put into practice the "theology of comfort" of which Paul spoke at the outset of this letter.

Optional Application: How can Paul's mix of exhortation and commendation be applied to your dealings with others?

_____

_____

_____

_____

2. In what ways did God comfort Paul (see 7:6-7)?

_____

_____

_____

_____

_____

The "tearful letter" and its effect (7:8-13)

3. Why were the Corinthians sorrowful (see 7:8)?

_____

_____

_____

4. a. Why did Paul initially regret sending the "tearful letter" to Corinth (see 7:8)?

_____

_____

_____

b. What made him change his attitude and not regret it in the end (see 7:8-9)?

_____

_____

_____

5. What do you think Paul meant by each of the qualities produced by the Corinthians' "godly sorrow" (7:11)?

earnestness _____

_____

_____

eagerness to clear yourselves _____

_____

_____

indignation _____

_____

_____

alarm _____

_____

_____

longing _____

_____

_____

concern _____

_____

_____

readiness to see justice done _____

_____

_____

_____

For Thought and Discussion: Share with the group an instance where someone disciplined you or spoke frankly with you in a manner which upset you at first, but later turned out for your benefit.

For Thought and Discussion: Describe a time when you have experienced worldly sorrow, and a time when you have experienced godly sorrow.

For Thought and Discussion: Discuss how Paul balanced warnings and exhortations with commendations in order to motivate the Corinthians to godly behavior.

6. How did the Corinthians prove themselves to "be innocent in this matter" (7:11)? By putting themselves right after earlier complicity in the wrong? By convincing Titus they had always

For Thought and Discussion: Who was the "injured party" (7:12)?

For Further Study: Read 2 Corinthians 7:8-13 alongside Hebrews 12:7-11 and Romans 8:17-18. Jot down ideas relating to the connection between spiritual growth and adversities.

been guiltless in the matter? Cite any textual evidence that supports your choice.

_____

_____

_____

_____

_____

Study Skill—Hebrew Thought Patterns

In 7:12 Paul draws what appears to be a sharp contrast between what prompted him to write the "tearful letter" and what did not motivate him to write it. In actual fact, however, it is not so much a contrast as it is a comparison. In other words, 7:12 might be paraphrased, "It was not so much on account of the one who did wrong or the injured party as it was that before God you could see for yourselves how devoted to us you are."

Paul's "tearful letter" was indeed concerned with the wrongdoer and the injured party, but that was not its purpose. Paul's chief concern was not with the individual parties, but with the entire church at Corinth and its relationship with him.

Hebrew thought patterns often draw such apparently sharp contrasts where in fact the writer is speaking of primary and secondary matters, as opposed to choosing one option at the expense of another. In the Old Testament, for example, God tells wayward Israel, "I desire mercy, not sacrifice" (Hosea 6:6). In so doing, God was not urging His people to abandon the sacrificial system He Himself had instituted, rather, He was saying, "Put first things first: mercy is even more important than sacrifice." In like manner, when Peter says that God is "not wanting anyone to perish, but everyone to come to repentance" (2 Peter 3:9), he is not implying that all people will be saved and no one will come to judgment. Rather, Peter is stating that what is closest to the heart of God is not judgment, but mercy.

7. What was the primary reason Paul wrote the "tearful letter" to Corinth (see 7:12)?

_____

_____

_____

_____

The relief of Titus (7:13-16)

8. Why do you think the Corinthians received Titus "with fear and trembling" (7:15)?

_____

_____

_____

_____

Your response

9. What aspect of 7:5-16 would you like to take to heart?

_____

_____

_____

_____

10. What would you like to do about this?

_____

_____

_____

_____

Optional Application: Ask God to point out one area in your life where you can follow Christ more closely so as not to embarrass (see 7:14) His name.

Optional Application: Is there someone whom you need to confront in a way that you hope will produce godly sorrow? What do you need to do? How can you do your part to make godly sorrow, rather than death-dealing sorrow, more likely?

11. List any questions you have about this passage.

_____

_____

_____

_____

For the group

Warm-up. Ask group members to share an incident where they felt a particular situation was almost certain to turn out badly, but ended up turning out well. How did they feel when they received the good news?

Read aloud and summarize.

Questions. Paul's relationship with the Corinthian church was volatile, to say the least! As you go through the questions in this section, try to get a feel for the dynamics of the human relationships reflected in Paul's words. What insights can you gain that you can apply to your relationships with family? Work? Church?

As you deal with Paul's words about godly sorrow, contrast the Corinthians' repentance with that of Judas, who felt anguish for having betrayed Jesus, but whose sorrow led not to salvation but to death (see Matthew 27:3-5). Discuss why it was not enough for Judas to feel sorry for his sins. What should he have done in order for his sorrow to be godly? Consider ways that your answers to these questions might apply to your own attitudes toward sin and toward Christ.

Wrap-up. Paul's final remark in this section is one of great confidence in the Corinthians (see 7:16), which puts him in good position to begin a positive appeal on behalf of the collection for the poor Christians in Jerusalem (see chapters 8 and 9).

Advise group members that lesson 9 is a long one. You may want to spend two weeks studying it, covering the first two sections the first week, with the final section and review the following week.

Worship.

Lesson Nine

2 CORINTHIANS 8:1-9:15

The Collection for the Saints at Jerusalem

Having expressed his confidence in the Corinthians, despite the rocky road their relationship has traveled in the past, Paul now builds upon the reconciliation between himself and the church at Corinth. He urges the Christians there to complete a task they had evidently begun earlier, but that had been sidetracked amid the controversies surrounding Paul's apostolic authority: the collection of funds for famine relief in Jerusalem.

In chapters 8–9, Paul makes it clear that the Corinthians' participation in the collection is as important for their spiritual welfare as it is for the physical welfare of the Christians in Jerusalem.

For Thought and Discussion: How can it be that "joy" coupled with "poverty" yields "generosity" (8:2)?

The need for the collection (8:1-15)

The Macedonian churches (8:1). This would include the churches at Philippi, Thessalonica, and Berea, to the north of Corinth.

1. What was the "grace" that God gave to the Macedonian Christians (8:1)?

_____

_____

_____

For Further Study:
As historical background for these chapters, read Acts 2:44-45; 4:34-35; 11:28-30; Romans 15:26; 1 Corinthians 16:1-4. In addition, consult commentaries or reference works if you wish. Determine why the church in Jerusalem was so poor at this time.

For Further Study:
Read Paul's letter to Titus. Then list the character traits that made Titus such a useful fellow worker.

Severe trial (8:2). Paul and Silas suffered violent opposition to their preaching of the gospel in Philippi, Thessalonica, and Berea (see Acts 16–17). Evidently many of the local residents continued to persecute the Christians in these churches in the same manner. Perhaps the "extreme poverty" mentioned in 8:2 refers to Christians whose families disinherited them after they decided to follow Christ.

Service to the Lord's people (8:4). See 1 Corinthians 16:1-3 and 2 Corinthians 8:10-11. This collection was for the poverty-stricken Jerusalem church. The extreme poverty of the church at Jerusalem was due in part to a famine mentioned by Luke in Acts 11:28-30.

2. What three things did the Macedonian Christians do that so impressed Paul (see 8:3-5)?

3. a. What had Titus "made a beginning" to do (8:6)?

b. What does his desire to continue tell us about his character?

4. Why is Paul so concerned not to command the Corinthians to participate in this collection (see 8:8)?

_____

_____

_____

_____

_____

Optional Application: Christ became poor on our behalf (see 8:9), and was therefore exalted by God (see Philippians 2:9-11). How can you follow His example?

5. When Paul says that Christ "became poor" for our sakes (8:9), what do you think he means?

_____

_____

_____

_____

_____

6. If the Corinthians were indeed the "first not only to give but also to have the desire to do so" (8:10), why did Paul use the actions of the Macedonian Christians—who did not give until later—as a means to motivate the Corinthians to give (see 8:11)?

_____

_____

_____

_____

_____

7. What do you think Paul means in 8:13 by the need for financial "equality" among Christians? Does he mean all Christians should have the same standard of living? Explain your view.

_____

_____

For Thought and Discussion: How was it that Paul and Titus shared the same concern for the Christians at Corinth (see 8:16)? How would you apply this to the task of doing Christian ministry today?

For Thought and Discussion: Why did Paul send two other Christians along with Titus to Corinth (see 8:18-23; 9:3-5), rather than just one (see Deuteronomy 19:15; Matthew 18:16)?

_____

_____

_____

The work connected with the collection (8:16–9:5)

8. Why do you think Paul felt it important to emphasize that Titus was traveling to Corinth not only on Paul's behalf, but also on his own initiative (see 8:17)?

_____

_____

_____

_____

The brother (8:18). *The NIV Study Bible* states, "Probably Luke, but possibly Barnabas. In any case, it was someone who was widely known for the faithfulness of his ministry."[1] Since Paul had broken with Barnabas several years earlier, however (see Acts 15:36-40), it is more likely that Barnabas was with John Mark in some other location.

Our brother (8:22). This Christian of good reputation, like the first "brother," remains anonymous.

---

9. Although Paul said "there is no need . . . to write" the Corinthians about this service to the Lord's people (9:1), nevertheless he did! What, then, did he feel he had to write them about? What was it that he did not need to write them about? (*Note*: In the original Greek, 9:1 begins with the word meaning "for" or "because.")

_____

_____

_____

10. What does 9:2-3 tell us about how Paul motivated the Macedonians to join in the collection for the Christians of Jerusalem?

_____

_____

_____

_____

The results of the collection (9:6-15)

11. Why do you think God loves a cheerful giver rather than one who gives great sums of money to charity under a sense of compulsion (see 9:7)?

_____

_____

_____

_____

12. a. In 9:9 Paul quotes Psalm 112:9. To whom does this Old Testament verse refer?

_____

_____

b. What is the point Paul is trying to make?

_____

_____

_____

_____

13. In the final analysis, what is the most important benefit Paul sees arising from this collection of money (see 9:12-14)?

For Thought and Discussion: Do you think Paul's teaching on giving in these chapters supports, refutes, or says nothing about the idea that Christians should give at least ten percent of their income to the church? Explain your view.

Optional Application: Would you say you are a generous giver? How can you grow in generosity?

Optional Application: What keeps you from being a cheerful giver? What can you do about this?

For Thought and Discussion: Discuss how Paul took pains to remain totally above board and accountable in his handling of the collection (see 8:20). How does this compare to the financial practices of Christian organizations today? What principles does Paul's approach offer us today?

_____

_____

_____

_____

14. What do Paul's words and actions regarding the collection for the Jerusalem church tell us about . . .

his strategy of motivating people to act?

_____

_____

_____

_____

_____

his views on holding people accountable for their handling of charitable funds?

_____

_____

_____

_____

the relationship Paul sees between Christian faith and giving?

_____

_____

_____

_____

15. How do you feel about the methods Paul used to motivate the Corinthians to participate in the collection?

_____

_____

_____

_____

Your response

16. How has your study of 2 Corinthians 8–9
affected your views on giving?

_____

_____

_____

_____

_____

17. How will you put into practice what Paul says in
these chapters?

_____

_____

_____

_____

18. List any questions you have about this passage.

_____

_____

_____

_____

_____

For the group

Warm-up. How do you feel when your pastor preaches about stewardship (money)?

Read aloud and summarize.

Questions. Whenever a preacher asks his congregation for money, things can get touchy! As you discuss this section, notice how Paul tries to motivate the Corinthians toward generosity, while at the same time not actually commanding them to take part in the collection.

The most famous verse in this section is 9:7, "God loves a cheerful giver." What does this mean? For example, does it mean God does not care how much we give, so long as we are cheerful in doing so? Or is it simply that, if it comes down to a choice between a small gift generously given and a larger gift somewhat begrudgingly given, God prefers the former? Be sure to deal with the spiritual principles that lie behind Paul's theology of giving.

Paul also takes care to make himself accountable to the Corinthians. Reflect on how his focus on financial accountability can be applied in your own lives and to the church today.

Wrap-up. In looking forward to the next session, encourage people to prepare by reading the four closing chapters of 2 Corinthians in their entirety. This sort of review will help underscore the marked shift in Paul's tone from chapters 1–9.

Worship.

1. Kenneth Barker, ed., *The NIV Study Bible* (Grand Rapids, MI: Zondervan, 1985), 1772.

2 CORINTHIANS 10:1-18

Paul Defends His Apostolic Ministry

Having urged the Christians at Corinth to remain obedient to his apostolic authority (see 1–7) and to participate in the collection of funds for the impoverished Jerusalem church (see 8–9), Paul now turns his attention more specifically to those in Corinth who have opposed his ministry. Although he addresses the entire congregation, his main burden in chapters 10–13 is not so much to persuade the Corinthians of his integrity (as it was in chapters 1–7) as it is to demonstrate his opponents' lack of apostolic credentials.

For Thought and Discussion: What emotions does chapter 10 express?

The power of Paul's ministry (10:1-11)

1. What is the source of Paul's power and authority in ministry (see 10:1)? Explain what you think his meaning is.

_____

_____

_____

_____

_____

_____

_____

Optional Application: Write down one way in which you can practice the meekness and gentleness of Christ in an important relationship.

2. How would you apply this to your own dealings with others?

_____

_____

_____

_____

_____

_____

I appeal to you . . . I beg you (10:1-2). The word translated "appeal" by the NIV is the same Greek word used in 2 Corinthians 1:4 when Paul speaks of the God who "comforts" Christians amid affliction. In addition, both *appeal* and *beg* are in the present tense ("I am appealing to you; I am begging you"), which may well indicate that Paul is referring not only to what he is going to say in chapters 10–13, but also to what he has already been saying in chapters 1–7, before he broke off to talk about the collection.

3. Paul's opponents accused him of carrying on his ministry "by the standards of this world" (10:2), that is, by merely human methods and ingenuity. List some of the standards that were falsely attributed to Paul by his opponents (see, for example, 1:17; 2:17; 3:5; 4:2; 7:2).

_____

_____

_____

_____

_____

4. From what you have read earlier in this letter, describe how the spiritual warfare Paul fights

and the spiritual weapons he uses differ from worldly warfare and weapons (see 10:3-4).

warfare _____

_____

_____

_____

_____

_____

weapons _____

_____

_____

_____

_____

_____

For Thought and Discussion: In Ephesians 6:17-18, Paul mentions two spiritual weapons: the Word of God and prayer. How are these relevant to the kind of warfare Paul talks about in 2 Corinthians 10?

For Thought and Discussion: Why would Paul wait to punish his opponents until after the rest of the Corinthians were solidly on his side?

For Further Study: In 2 Corinthians 10:4 Paul mentions spiritual weapons. Make a list of the weapons he speaks of in Ephesians 6:11-18.

Every thought (10:5). Many people interpret Paul as talking here about his inner battle, striving to force all of his thoughts to be pleasing to Christ. However, the paragraph as a whole is clearly not about Paul's inner life, but the way he goes about the apostolic job of spreading the gospel and supervising the churches he has planted. The war he speaks of is the war to demolish strongholds in *other people's* lives and to take *other people's* thoughts captive to help them become obedient to Christ. That doesn't mean it's unimportant to take our own thoughts captive, but this doesn't happen to be what Paul is talking about here.

While his opponents seek to spread their "gospel" and their authority through effective public relations techniques, charisma, and other worldly weapons of persuasion, Paul sees his task as primarily a spiritual battle waged through hard work, integrity, prayer, and above all, reliance on the power of the Holy Spirit (compare 1 Corinthians 2:1-5).

Optional Application: Do you tend to fight with worldly weapons or spiritual ones? How could you use spiritual weapons to accomplish what is currently facing you?

For Thought and Discussion: What can 10:1-6 teach a pastor or elder about how to exercise spiritual authority?

Complete (10:6). Paul probably doesn't mean he's waiting until every person associated with the Corinthian church submits to his apostolic authority. Rather, he will punish the disobedience of a stubborn few when the vast majority of the Corinthians, in whom he already has a measure of confidence, finally return that confidence in full by acknowledging his authority.

5. If we wanted to use Paul's methods to spread the gospel, how could we go about taking people's thoughts captive through spiritual means?

_____

_____

_____

_____

_____

_____

6. Paul chides the Corinthians for evaluating both himself and his opponents on the basis of external qualities (see 10:7). List several specific ways in which people today tend to judge leaders by "looking only on the surface of things" as opposed to looking for qualities of true worth.

looking on the surface _____

_____

_____

_____

_____

_____

_____

true worth (below the surface) _____

_____

_____

_____

_____

_____

_____

7. Why are we so often attracted to leaders who look good on the surface rather than to leaders like Paul?

_____

_____

_____

_____

_____

Optional Application: As you assess your leaders, are you looking on the surface or beneath it? What can you do about that?

Belong to Christ (10:7). From the context we can see that Paul is not talking about being a Christian but about having apostolic authority directly from Christ.

For building you up rather than tearing you down (10:8). Paul contrasts his ministry with that of his opponents. He is probably comparing the results of his ministry to theirs, though he may also have in mind the difference between his methods and those of his opponents: Paul pleads with the "humility and gentleness of Christ" (10:1), while his opponents lord over the Corinthians and may even go so far as to strike them (see 11:20).

8. Why would Paul's opponents try to convince the Corinthians that Paul's "letters are weighty and forceful, but in person he is unimpressive and his speaking amounts to nothing" (10:10)?

_____

_____

_____

_____

For Further Study:
Read Acts 15:1-35.
Summarize the principal issue at stake at the church conference in Jerusalem.

For Further Study:
Compare Romans 15:20-24 with 2 Corinthians 10:15-16. Write down what you learn about Paul's missionary strategy.

The scope of Paul's ministry (10:12-18)

9. What do you think it means to "measure themselves by themselves and compare themselves with themselves" (10:12)?

_____

_____

_____

_____

_____

_____

The sphere of service God himself has assigned to us (10:13). God had led Paul to Corinth, and he viewed his opponents' attempts to usurp his authority there as encroachment upon his field of ministry. If Paul's opponents were Palestinian Jewish Christians intent on introducing legalistic teachings among the Gentiles, Paul's language here may also refer to agreements mentioned in Acts 15:24-29 and Galatians 2:1-10 that authorized Paul to preach his gospel to the Gentiles and prohibited Jewish Christians from inducing Gentiles to submit to circumcision and the Law of Moses.

10. Why was Paul justified in boasting about the spiritual growth of the Corinthian Christians, whereas Paul's opponents were not (see 10:13-16)?

_____

_____

_____

_____

_____

11. Why was Paul so eager to see the Corinthian Christians grow into a strong, self-sufficient church (see 10:15-16)?

_____

_____

_____

_____

_____

For Thought and Discussion: Has anyone ever tried to boast about or take credit for work you did? If so, how did it make you feel?

12. What is "boast[ing] in the Lord" (10:17)?

_____

_____

_____

_____

13. Why do you think Paul endorses "boast[ing] in the Lord" but censures all other forms of boasting?

_____

_____

_____

_____

14. Summarize the differences you see between Paul's ministry on one hand, and that of his opponents on the other.

_____

_____

_____

_____

_____

Your response

15. What stands out to you in this passage?

_____

_____

_____

_____

16. What difference would you like this to make in your life?

_____

_____

_____

_____

17. List any questions you have about this passage.

_____

_____

_____

_____

_____

For the group

Warm-up. Have you ever had someone try to undermine your reputation? How did that feel?

Read aloud and summarize.

Questions. Beginning with chapter 10, Paul's tone takes on an urgency and intensity reflected only sporadically in chapters 1–9. Paul has already spelled out the nature and goals of his ministry, including the heart of the gospel message itself. Group members should therefore discuss why, after doing all this, he feels compelled to spend so much additional time attacking his opponents.

Some people may express misgivings about Paul's increasingly sharp tone in chapters 10–13. You may want to ponder just why the apostle felt so incensed. Pose these two questions, for example: "Have you ever done something noteworthy for which someone else then tried to take credit? If so, how did you feel about the person who tried to take credit for your work?" As group members reflect on these questions, it should put Paul's deep feelings of indignation into their proper perspective (refer also to the note on 10:13).

Leadership is hard work. And leadership in the church is especially difficult because our battle is not merely against people, but against spiritual forces (see Ephesians 6:10-17). Discuss the contrast between "worldly weapons" and "spiritual weapons" Paul refers to in 10:3-5.

Wrap-up. In 10:17 Paul says, "let the one who boasts boast in the Lord." In preparing for the next two lessons, have group members consider why it is proper to "boast in the Lord," but not to boast in anything else.

Worship.

Lesson Eleven

2 CORINTHIANS 11:1-21

Paul Chastises His Opponents

Up to this point Paul has largely avoided direct attacks against his opponents. Instead, he has either argued against their legalistic theology (see 3:6–5:21) or made indirect criticisms of their activities (see 10:1-18). Beginning with chapter 11, however, the attack becomes sharper even than in chapter 10, as Paul pulls out all the stops in a concluding crescendo designed to overwhelm his opponents once and for all.

For Further Study:
Read Exodus 20:4-5. What does it mean for God to be a "jealous" God?

Paul's jealousy for the Corinthians

(11:1-6)

1. To what does Paul refer when he asks the Corinthians to bear with his "foolishness" (11:1)?

_____

_____

_____

_____

2. Write out a definition of *jealousy*. How does the "godly jealousy" that Paul feels toward the Corinthians (11:2) differ from worldly jealousy?

_____

_____

_____

_____

_____

3. a. In 11:3, Paul refers to Eve and the serpent. To what desire did the serpent appeal in order to lead Eve astray (see Genesis 3:1-6)?

_____

_____

_____

_____

b. What does this tell you about the tactics of Paul's opponents in Corinth?

_____

_____

_____

_____

4. Paul's first reason for asking the Corinthians to bear with him is his "godly jealousy" (11:2) for them. What is his second reason for asking them to put up with his boasting (see 11:4)?

_____

_____

_____

Those "super-apostles" (11:5). Literally, "the superlative apostles." Paul could be referring to either of two groups here: his opponents at Corinth, or the chief apostles of the church in Jerusalem (James, Peter, and John, for example).

At first glance it appears Paul is making a sarcastic reference to his opponents at Corinth, who boast of their own achievements (see 10:12) and use high-handed tactics in dealing with the church (see 11:20). They may be "super" in their own eyes, but Paul does not feel "in the least inferior" (11:5) to them (again, a bit of sarcasm, this time by way of understatement).

Some commentators, however, find it hard to believe that Paul would stoop so low as to compare himself to his opponents, even by way of irony or sarcasm.[1] Instead, they see here a reference to the original twelve apostles, or to the chief apostles of that group. These commentators believe that Paul's opponents at Corinth were attacking his apostolic status by claiming Paul to be inferior to the Twelve. Indeed, perhaps Paul's opponents were Palestinian Jewish Christians who claimed to be speaking for the Twelve.

If this be the case, the situation here is similar to that alluded to in Galatians 2:9, where Paul uses the mildly ironic (not sarcastic) term "those esteemed as pillars" to speak of James, Peter, and John, in order to make clear to the Galatians that he is not inferior to them. Thus Paul's reference to the "superlative" or "chief" apostles in 2 Corinthians 11:5 would be Paul's way of telling the Corinthians, as he did the Galatians earlier, that he is in no way a "second-class" apostle.

It is impossible to know which of these two very different groups Paul had in mind. The immediate context of 11:5 favors the first alternative (Paul's opponents at Corinth) for at least two reasons: (1) The verse immediately following obviously refers to a criticism of Paul made by his opponents (why would the Twelve deride Paul's lack of oratorical skills?); and (2) Paul does compare himself to his opponents (albeit ironically) just a few paragraphs later in 11:22–12:10. On the other hand, there is precedent (see Galatians 2:1-10) for those opposing Paul to downgrade him by comparing him to the Twelve. And Paul's only other reference to the "super-apostles," in 2 Corinthians 12:11, could refer to the Twelve in that context.

For Further Study:
Read Acts 18:1-5 and
1 Corinthians 9:1-18
for further insight into
the way Paul dealt
with the delicate mat-
ter of financial sup-
port for his ministry.

**For Thought and
Discussion:** At which
points should we
today follow Paul's
procedures for finan-
cial support and
accountability (see
2 Corinthians 11:7-12)?

5. In 11:6 Paul refers to a specific criticism his
   opponents made of him in order to denigrate
   his authority. What was this criticism, and how
   does Paul respond to it?

   _____

   _____

   _____

   _____

Financial independence (11:7-12)

6. In spite of what Paul had written earlier to the
   Corinthians (see 1 Corinthians 9:3-18), what
   other criticism did Paul's opponents make
   to argue that he was not a true apostle (see
   2 Corinthians 11:7)?

   _____

   _____

I robbed other churches (11:8). Again, Paul's sharp
   irony comes through with his use of the word
   robbed. Traveling teachers who were concerned
   about their reputation would often work at
   a trade, as did Paul when he first arrived at
   Corinth (see Acts 18:1-4). When Silas and Timo-
   thy arrived from Macedonia, however, they evidently brought the financial support to which
   Paul alludes here (see 2 Corinthians 11:8-9),
   for Paul then quit making tents and began full-
   time preaching and teaching (see Acts 18:5).

7. Why do you think Paul was willing to accept
   financial support from Macedonian Christians
   while he was ministering at Corinth, but
   was unwilling to accept support from the
   Corinthians themselves (see 11:8-12)?

   _____

   _____

_____

_____

_____

False apostles (11:13-15)

8. What sorts of "masquerades" (see 11:13-15) did Paul's opponents use to deceive the Corinthians? (Review what Paul has said about his opponents up to this point.)

_____

_____

_____

_____

_____

9. Make a list of those qualities that you believe should characterize a true minister of Christ, as opposed to those qualities that are typical of false ministers of Christ.

true ministers _____

_____

_____

_____

_____

false ministers _____

_____

_____

_____

_____

_____

For Thought and Discussion: How do modern-day false apostles (those claiming spiritual authority they do not possess) try to deceive Christians and gather a following? How can Christians discern such people and resist them?

Optional Application: List some specific steps you can take in order to avoid being deceived by Satan (see 11:14-15).

Playing the fool (11:16-21)

10. a. Who are the "fools" Paul refers to in 11:16-19?

_____

_____

_____

b. What, then, does Paul mean when he says, "Let no one take me for a fool" (11:16)?

_____

_____

_____

_____

11. What sort of "boasting" characterizes the "fool" (11:17)? How does this differ from boasting "in the Lord" (10:17)?

_____

_____

_____

_____

Your response

12. In summary, why is Paul so angry?

_____

_____

_____

_____

13. What does 11:1-21 tell you about Paul as a person?

_____

_____

_____

_____

14. What would you like to take to heart from 11:1-21?

_____

_____

_____

_____

15. List any questions you have about this passage.

_____

_____

_____

_____

For the group

Warm-up. Name a situation in which you feel a tension between tolerance and Christian conviction.

Read aloud and summarize.

Questions. The word *jealousy* (see 11:2) brings forth images of intolerance and selfishness. Yet the Bible says that God is a jealous God. As the group deals with question 2, try to reach some consensus as to what sort of jealousy is godly and good, and what sort of jealousy is harmful. (It's interesting to note that the people Jesus and Paul tolerated the least were those who used a system of rules to decide who was in and who was out.)

Question 3 deals with the important subject of how Satan attempts to deceive Christians and subvert their faith. Read 1 John 2:16, and discuss specific means Satan uses to ruin our faith in Christ, and specific countermeasures we can take to oppose him. You will find it helpful to review Ephesians 6:10-17.

Paul's opponents at Corinth were not only attacking him (see 2 Corinthians 11:5-6), but were arrogant in their treatment of the Corinthians (see 11:19-20). Why do you think some people at Corinth—as well as some today—respond so readily to leaders who are strong to the point of being high-handed? How can Christians strike a proper balance between proper obedience to authority on the one hand, and discerning evaluation of their leaders on the other?

In 11:20-21 Paul cites one difference between the leadership exercised by his opponents and his own style of leadership. Discuss other specific differences you believe should characterize godly leadership as opposed to worldly leadership.

Wrap-up. In the upcoming lesson we find Paul finally making use of one of his opponents' favorite tactics: boasting. As you read 11:21–12:13, consider why Paul felt it necessary to do this, and in what respects his boasting differs from theirs.

Worship.

1. See, for example, Murray J. Harris, *2 Corinthians*, The Expositor's Bible Commentary, vol. 10, ed. Frank E. Gaebelein (Grand Rapids, MI: Zondervan, 1976), 386. See also C. K. Barrett, *The Second Epistle to the Corinthians* (New York: Harper & Row, 1973), 277–278.

2 CORINTHIANS 11:21–12:13

Boasting in Weakness

Although Paul has talked about boasting throughout this letter, he has been reluctant to do it. But now he feels compelled, both by his opponents' self-glorification and the Corinthians' obvious tendency to be swayed by such theatrics, to match the false apostles' claims, and to add a new twist—boasting in weakness—to this contest for bragging rights at Corinth.

More perils of Paul (11:21-33)

1. What do you think Paul means by the phrase "speaking as a fool" (11:21)?

_____

_____

_____

_____

_____

Hebrews . . . Israelites . . . Abraham's descendants (11:22). Paul's opponents took pride in their Jewish heritage—a heritage which Paul shared, but which he refused to claim as any sort of spiritual merit badge as his opponents evidently did. This verse indicates that they were "Judaizers"—Jews (whether professing Christians or not, we cannot be certain)

For Further Study:
Paul evidently encountered similar opponents in Macedonia (see Philippians 3:2-6). In each case, what were Paul's opponents teaching the new Christians? How did Paul oppose these false teachers?

who taught that one had to follow certain distinctive Jewish practices as an essential sign of one's true faith in God.

2. How does Paul's boasting change following his insistence that "I have worked much harder" (11:23)?

_____

_____

_____

_____

_____

Forty lashes minus one . . . beaten with rods . . . pelted with stones . . . shipwrecked (11:24-25). Forty lashes was a Jewish form of punishment (see Deuteronomy 25:1-3), but the Jews always limited it to thirty-nine, so as not to break the Law should they miscount. "Beaten with rods" on the other hand, refers to Roman punishment (see Acts 16:22-23). Jews stoned people in order to kill, not merely punish, them.

In the book of Acts, Luke records none of the floggings Paul mentions, and only one of the beatings by Rome. The stoning probably refers to Acts 14:19. Luke does mention one shipwreck, but it occurred after Paul wrote this passage (see Acts 27:13-44). However, Paul traveled more than a thousand miles by ship, and wrecks were frequent.

3. What point is Paul trying to make by the things he boasts about in 11:24-26?

_____

_____

_____

_____

_____

4. From 11:29, how would you put into your own words Paul's attitude toward . . .

those Christians at Corinth who were weak in their faith?

_____

_____

_____

_____

those who led such weak Christians into sin?

_____

_____

_____

_____

King Aretas (11:32). Aretas IV, father-in-law of Herod Antipas, ruled over the kingdom of the Nabataean Arabs (which included Damascus) from about 9 BC to AD 40. Either the king or his governor at Damascus may have been offended by Paul's evangelistic activity there, perhaps because it threatened domestic tranquillity by offending the Jews of the region. Paul's fourteen years in Arabia (Nabataea; see Galatians 1:17) was more than a time of spiritual reflection; Luke makes it clear that Paul was proclaiming Jesus as the Messiah from the moment of his conversion (see Acts 9:20).

The vision and the thorn (12:1-10)

5. a. Why is Paul reluctant to talk about the vision he had fourteen years earlier (see 12:3-6)?

_____

_____

_____

Optional Application: What "thorns" in your life (physical or other afflictions) do you feel God could use to His glory? If you feel this is not yet happening in your life or that God is not yet being glorified in your weakness, what obstacles lie in the way of that happening?

For Further Study: Read Isaiah 64:4. What makes the God of Israel different from all other gods? How does this tie in with what Paul is trying to teach the Corinthians?

For Thought and Discussion: How do 11:30 and 12:10 reflect the theme of the entire letter?

_____

_____

b. Why do you think he mentions it?

_____

_____

_____

_____

Third heaven . . . paradise (12:2,4). In Jewish thought, this was the abode of the righteous dead. The Jews distinguished between the "first paradise" (see Genesis 2–3); the "last paradise" (see Revelation 2:7); and the "hidden paradise" (see Matthew 13:44), which exists during the time between the first and last paradise.

Thorn in my flesh (12:7). We do not know what this affliction was. On the basis of Galatians 4:15 and 6:11, some have speculated that Paul had problems with his vision.

6. In 12:7 Paul says, "I was given a thorn in my flesh." Who was responsible for giving Paul this physical affliction: God or Satan? Explain your answer.

_____

_____

_____

_____

_____

7. How could Paul affirm the apparent paradox, "When I am weak, then I am strong" (12:10)?

_____

_____

_____

_____

_____

8. Write down one way in which you have seen Christ's power revealed through either your own weakness, or the weakness of someone else.

_____

_____

_____

_____

_____

The need to be foolish (12:11-13)

9. What does Paul's reluctance to boast (see 12:11) tell you about . . .

his character? _____

_____

_____

_____

_____

_____

his concern for the Corinthians? _____

_____

_____

_____

_____

_____

For Thought and Discussion: Paul speaks of "signs, wonders and miracles" in 12:12 as being the marks of an apostolic ministry. What role do you think such things should play in evangelism today? Explain.

For Thought and Discussion: Why do you think Paul boasted in his sufferings rather than in the signs and wonders he apparently performed?

Your response

10. If you were one of the Corinthian Christians, how would you feel about Paul after reading 10:1–12:13?

_____

_____

_____

_____

_____

11. How do Paul's remarks in 11:21–12:13 reflect the themes of the entire letter?

_____

_____

_____

_____

_____

12. What statement of Paul's in this passage would you like to take to heart?

_____

_____

_____

_____

_____

13. How will you apply this insight to your life?

_____

_____

_____

_____

_____

14. List any questions you have about 11:21–12:13.

_____

_____

_____

_____

_____

For the group

Warm-up. How important do you believe status is in the church today? What sorts of things give a person status?

Read aloud and summarize.

Questions. Paul uses the word *fool* frequently in this section. Talk about why Paul regards his status-seeking opponents as foolish. What is there about striving for status in the church that is contrary to God's will for our lives?

Paul also speaks of the "pressure" of his concern for the churches (11:28). Discuss some of the pressures your pastor must be under in trying to lead the congregation. How can you, as a church member, be supportive?

Question 6 goes to the heart of the problem of evil. In Paul's mind, God is sovereign, and nothing happens outside His will. God is also the "God of all comfort" (1:3). Yet evil exists, even in the life of a Christian, and sometimes prayer does not take it away (sec 12:8). As a group, discuss why God permitted affliction in Paul's life in this specific instance (see 12:7-10). Then—if you feel venturesome!—talk about broader aspects of the problem of evil. (Some group members may feel very strongly about this, perhaps because of afflictions they have suffered or are currently undergoing. Be sensitive to this, and remind everyone that Christ underwent the most horrible, undeserved affliction of all time—on our behalf [see 5:21]. In the final analysis, Christ Himself—and not some sophisticated argument—is God's answer to the problem of evil.)

Question 11 deals with the overall theme of 2 Corinthians. Be sure to allow time for the group to share their responses. If you run out of time this week, include it in next week's discussion.

Wrap-up. Next week's lesson is the final one in this study guide. Encourage group members to think about where they would like to go from here. (Directly into another LifeChange study? Take a break? Meet for an additional week after lesson 13 to review the entire study? Or perhaps have a social event at the end of the study, in celebration of getting through this very difficult letter of Paul.)

Worship.

2 CORINTHIANS 12:14-13:14

Final Appeal, Admonitions, and Farewell

Having finished his exhortation to the wayward
Corinthians, Paul now anticipates his third visit
to that church. His final appeal makes it clear that
he does not want a repeat of his second, "painful"
visit—the visit that occasioned the "tearful letter"
mentioned earlier (see 2:4).

This final section exhibits the same tension
Paul finds himself in throughout 2 Corinthians, as
he seeks a proper balance between nurturing love
and chastening discipline, which are his respon-
sibilities as a spiritual father to the Corinthian
Christians.

No burden except love (12:14-18)

1. Why is Paul determined not to be a financial
   burden to the Corinthians (see 12:14)?

   _____

   _____

   _____

2. How should they respond to this demonstration
   of love (see 12:15)?

   _____

   _____

   _____

Trickery (12:16). Even though all the Corinthians, including Paul's opponents, would agree with his claim that "I have not been a [financial] burden to you," some evidently went on to argue in this manner: "It may be true that Paul himself took no money—*yet*, Paul *did* commission others, such as Titus, to do this for him, and for his own profit, under the pretense of taking up a collection for the poor in Jerusalem."

Paul replies that the Corinthians know Titus' integrity full well, and with the fact that Titus was held accountable by another Christian evidently known to the Corinthians ("our brother"; compare 8:18). Titus' visit to Corinth, which Paul mentions here, could be either the visit on which Titus commenced the collection (see 8:6), or the visit when he completed it (see 8:16-24).

3. Why was financial integrity so important to Paul?

_____

_____

_____

_____

_____

Fears about the unrepentant (12:19-21)

4. This letter to the Corinthians has often been called a "personal apologetics" or self-defense. How would Paul respond to that (see 12:19)?

_____

_____

_____

_____

_____

5. What three fears concerning his upcoming visit prompted Paul to write 2 Corinthians (see 12:20-21)?

_____

_____

_____

_____

_____

Selfish ambition (12:20). Paul is most likely referring to matters he discussed in 1 Corinthians 1:10-31 and 1 Corinthians 12-14. The church at Corinth was riddled with factions, driven by selfish ambition, trying to play spiritual one-upmanship with each other. Paul countered this prideful attitude by admonishing them to boast only in what Christ had done for them (see 1 Corinthians 1:31; compare 2 Corinthians 10:17).

My God will humble me (12:21). Perhaps "humiliate" would be a better translation. Also, the word *again* in 12:21 should be seen as applying to "my God will humble me" in addition to "when I come again."

Paul was evidently humiliated by one or more of his opponents during his second visit to Corinth (the "painful visit"). Perhaps this incident helped impress upon him the truth that "we have this treasure [that is, the gospel ministry] in jars of clay" (4:7). However, the fact that Paul learned a valuable lesson from this experience did not make him want to go through it again!

Impurity . . . debauchery (12:21). Paul first dealt with this subject in 1 Corinthians 5. The fact that sexual immorality was still rampant in Corinth even as Paul wrote 2 Corinthians makes it unlikely that the person Paul was willing to forgive was guilty of sexual misconduct (see 2:5; 1 Corinthians 6:1-5). It is doubtful that Paul would single out one instance of such behavior if it was common.

For Thought and Discussion:

a. In 12:20 Paul lists a number of sins of which the Corinthians had been guilty. Why are these so serious? Why are they so common in the church? What are healthy ways of dealing with such behavior?

b. Paul lists sexual sins in 12:21. Do you think these are more serious than the sins he lists in 12:20? Why or why not?

A stern admonition (13:1-4)

6. To whom or what do you think Paul refers in the phrase "two or three witnesses" (13:1)? Is it (a) Paul's three visits to Corinth, which together comprise a threefold witness that would bring certain justice to those still in rebellion against Paul's authority, or (b) the legal strictness that would apply to any investigation Paul or the assembled church (see Matthew 13:15-20; 1 Corinthians 5:3-5) would conduct at Corinth to discipline disobedience? Explain.

_____

_____

_____

_____

_____

7. When Paul says that Christ "was crucified in weakness" (13:4), do you think he is referring to the weakness of the physical suffering Christ endured on the cross or the weakness of Christ's refusal to retaliate against His persecutors (as in Matthew 26:53)? Which of these two options is more consistent with Paul's next statement, "Likewise, we are weak in him"?

_____

_____

_____

_____

Examine yourselves! (13:5-10)

Test yourselves (13:5). The Greek verb here (_dokimazo_) is derived from the noun translated "proof" (_dokime_) in 13:3. This sort of "test" or "proof" does not look for faults to disqualify someone, but rather it seeks out the good, it makes a person qualified for a particular task or role. Paul's plea for self-examination is thus not a call for the Corinthians to go on a legalistic witch hunt. Rather, Paul is urging each professing Christian at Corinth to see if his or her life does indeed possess a significant measure of the power and love of Jesus Christ.

Unless . . . you fail the test (13:5). Paul realized that the mark of true Christianity was not merely a past profession of faith, but the present work of the Holy Spirit in one's life.

   Because Paul's exhortation here is a call to examination, it is unlikely that Paul expected anyone in the Corinthian church to conclude that he or she had "failed the test" (i.e., was not a Christian). The Corinthians, after all, were not known for their spiritual discernment! It is more likely that Paul included this statement to introduce 13:6. In this way he would be saying in effect, "If you examine your lives and find yourselves to be in Christ, I hope you will come to the obvious conclusion that I am Christ's apostle—since I'm the one who preached Christ to you in the first place."

For Thought and Discussion: What sort of criteria or "test" (13:5-6) should Christians use to verify that they are indeed "in Christ"?

For Thought and Discussion: Share with the group an incident where you had trouble finding a proper balance between nurturing love and necessary discipline.

8. What does 13:7 tell you about Paul's concern for . . .

the Corinthians' spiritual welfare? _____ _

_____

_____

_____

_____

his own reputation? _____

_____

_____

_____

_____

9. Why did Paul write 2 Corinthians (see 13:10)?

_____

_____

_____

_____

_____

Conclusion (13:11-14)

Strive for full restoration (13:11). The single Greek word translated by this phrase means "to mend, to restore."

10. Write out a paraphrase of 13:11.

_____

_____

_____

_____

_____

_____

Your response

11. What remaining questions do you have about 2 Corinthians?

_____

_____

_____

_____

12. What is the most significant thing you learned from studying this letter?

_____

_____

_____

_____

_____

13. If you received this letter, how would you respond?

_____

_____

_____

_____

14. What do you think would be an appropriate response for you to make now?

_____

_____

_____

_____

For the group

Warm-up. Ask group members to share briefly what one quality of Paul's most impressed them as they studied 2 Corinthians.

Read aloud and summarize.

Questions. As you complete your study of 2 Corinthians, have group members review and discuss the principal themes, and talk about Paul's purpose or purposes in writing this letter.

In both 1 and 2 Corinthians Paul addresses the problem of factionalism (see, for example, 2 Corinthians 12:20). Why are factions so dangerous to a church? What can be done to prevent them?

Paul concludes this letter by urging the Corinthians to examine themselves to see whether or not they have truly committed their lives to Christ. Each group member should pose the same question to himself or herself. Perhaps some people began the study as inquirers, not yet having trusted in Christ as Lord and Savior, but would now like to do so. Encourage them without being pushy.

Summarize. Recap both this week's lesson, and the thrust of the entire book. You may want to add your own insights gained during the study to what is written in the introduction and the overview found in lesson 1. Urge group members to feel free to volunteer insights they have gained during the course of the study.

Wrap-up. Talk about what group members would like to do as a group now that this study is complete (see "Wrap-up" section, lesson 12, for some ideas). Also, have people share one new truth they gained from 2 Corinthians during the course of the study, and how they are going to apply that to their lives in the weeks to come.

Worship.

STUDY AIDS

For further information on the material covered in this study, consider the following sources. If your local bookstore does not have them, you can ask the bookstore to order them from the publishers, or you can find them in a public university or seminary library. If they are out of print, you might be able to find them online.

Commentaries on 2 Corinthians

Barrett, C. K. *The Second Epistle to the Corinthians* (Harper & Row, 1973).
A scholarly work that deals in-depth with all of the major issues. Not light reading, but worth the effort. Barrett believes Paul wrote chapters 10–13 after chapters 1–9.

Bruce, F. F. *1 and 2 Corinthians* (Oliphants, 1971).
Bruce, probably the premier English-speaking New Testament scholar, is also accessible and readable.

Harris, Murray J. *2 Corinthians*, The Expositor's Bible Commentary, volume 10, edited by Frank E. Gaebelein (Zondervan, 1976).
Well suited for the lay reader, it nevertheless discusses the pertinent issues. Generally conservative in its conclusions.

Hughes, P. E. *Paul's Second Epistle to the Corinthians* (Eerdmans, 1962).
Written by an evangelical scholar who holds to the unity of the letter.

Historical and background sources

Bruce, F. F. *New Testament History* (Doubleday, 1979).
A readable history of Herodian kings, Roman governors, philosophical schools, Jewish sects, Jesus, the early Jerusalem church, Paul, and early gentile Christianity. Well documented with footnotes for the serious student, but the notes do not intrude.

Gundry, Robert H. *A Survey of the New Testament*, revised edition (Zondervan, 1981).
An evangelically-oriented survey designed for college undergraduates. It includes maps, charts, outlines, reading lists, and study questions. The best book of its kind.

Harrison, E. F. *Introduction to the New Testament* (Eerdmans, 1971).
History from Alexander the Great—who made Greek culture
dominant in the biblical world—through philosophies, pagan and Jewish
religions, Jesus' ministry and teaching (the weakest section), and the
spread of Christianity. Very good maps and photographs of the land, art,
and architecture of New Testament times.

Packer, James I., Merril C. Tenney, William White, Jr. *The Bible Almanac*
(Thomas Nelson, 1980).
One of the most accessible handbooks of the people of the Bible and
how they lived. Many photos and illustrations liven an already readable text.

Histories, concordances, dictionaries, and handbooks

A **concordance** lists words of the Bible alphabetically along with each verse in
which the word appears. It lets you do your own word studies. An *exhaustive
concordance* lists every word used in a given translation, while an *abridged*
or *complete concordance* omits either some words, some occurrences of the
word, or both.

Two of the three best exhaustive concordances are the venerable *Strong's
Exhaustive Concordance* and *Young's Analytical Concordance to the Bible*.
Both are available based on the King James Version and the New American
Standard Bible. *Strong's* has an index in which you can find out which Greek
or Hebrew word is used in a given English verse (although its information
is occasionally outdated). *Young's* breaks up each English word it translates.
Neither concordance requires knowledge of the original languages.

Perhaps the best exhaustive concordance currently on the market is *The
NIV Exhaustive Concordance*. It features a Hebrew-to-English and a Greek-
to-English lexicon (based on the eclectic text underlying the NIV), which are
also keyed to *Strong's* numbering system.

Among other good, less expensive concordances, *Cruden's Complete
Concordance* is keyed to the King James and Revised Versions, the *NIV
Complete Concordance* is keyed to the New International Version. These
include all references to every word included, but they omit "minor" words.
They also lack indexes to the original languages.

A **Bible dictionary** or **Bible encyclopedia** alphabetically lists articles
about people, places, doctrines, important words, customs, and geography of
the Bible.

The New Bible Dictionary edited by J. D. Douglas, F. F. Bruce, J. I.
Packer, N. Hillyer, D. Guthrie, A. R. Millard, and D. J. Wiseman (Tyndale,
1982) is more comprehensive than most dictionaries. Its 1,300 pages include
quantities of information along with excellent maps, charts, diagrams, and
an index for cross-referencing.

Unger's Bible Dictionary by Merrill F. Unger (Moody, 1979) is equally
good and is available in an inexpensive paperback edition.

The Zondervan Pictorial Encyclopedia edited by Merrill C. Tenney
(Zondervan, 1975, 1976) is excellent and exhaustive, and has been revised
and updated. Its five 1,000-page volumes represent a significant financial

investment, however, and all but very serious students may prefer to use it at a church, public college, or seminary library.

Unlike a Bible dictionary in the above sense, *Vine's Expository Dictionary of New Testament Words* by W. E. Vine (various publishers) alphabetically lists major words used in the King James Version and defines each New Testament Greek word that the KJV translates with its English word. *Vine's* also lists verse references where that Greek word appears, so you can do your own cross-references and word studies without knowing any Greek.

Vine's is a good, basic book for beginners, but it is much less complete than other Greek helps for English speakers. More serious students might prefer *The New International Dictionary of New Testament Theology* edited by Colin Brown (Zondervan) or *The Theological Dictionary of the New Testament* by Gerhard Kittel and Gerhard Friedrich, abridged in one volume by Geoffrey W. Bromiley (Eerdmans).

A **Bible atlas** can be a great aid to understanding what is going on in a book of the Bible and how geography affected events. Here are a few good choices.

The Macmillan Atlas by Yohanan Aharoni and Michael Avi-Yonah (Macmillan, 1968, 1977) contains 264 maps, 89 photos, and 12 graphics. The many maps of individual events portray battles, movements of people, and changes of boundaries in detail.

The New Bible Atlas by J. J. Bimson and J. P. Kane (Tyndale, 1985) has 73 maps, 34 photos, and 34 graphics. Its evangelical perspective, concise and helpful text, and excellent research make it a very good choice, but its greatest strength lies in outstanding graphics, such as cross-sections of the Dead Sea.

The Bible Mapbook by Simon Jenkins (Lion, 1984) is much shorter and less expensive than most other atlases, so it offers a good first taste of the usefulness of maps. It contains 91 simple maps, very little text, and 20 graphics. Some of the graphics are computer-generated and intriguing.

The Moody Atlas of Bible Lands by Barry J. Beitzel (Moody, 1984) is scholarly, evangelical, and full of theological text, indexes, and references. This admirable reference work will be too deep and costly for some, but Beitzel shows vividly how God prepared the land of Israel perfectly for the acts of salvation He planned to accomplish in it.

A **handbook** of biblical customs can also be useful. Two good ones are *Today's Handbook of Bible Times and Customs* by William L. Coleman (Bethany, 1984) and the less detailed *Daily Life in Bible Times* (Nelson, 1982).

For small-group leaders

Barker, Steve, et al. *The Small Group Leader's Handbook* (InterVarsity, 1982).
 Written by an InterVarsity small group with college students primarily in mind. It includes information on small-group dynamics and how to lead in light of them, and many ideas for worship, building community, and outreach. It has a good chapter on doing inductive Bible study.

Griffin, Em. *Getting Together: A Guide for Good Groups* (InterVarsity, 1982).
 Applies to all kinds of groups, not just Bible studies. From his own experience, Griffin draws deep insights into why people join groups; how

people relate to each other; and principles of leadership, decision making, and discussions. It is fun to read, but its 229 pages will take more time than the above book.

Hunt, Gladys. *You Can Start a Bible Study Group* (Harold Shaw, 1984).
Builds on Hunt's thirty years of experience leading groups. This book is wonderfully focused on God's enabling. It is both clear and applicable for Bible study groups of all kinds.

McBride, Neal F. *How to Build a Small Groups Ministry* (NavPress, 1994).
This hands-on workbook for pastors and lay leaders includes everything you need to know to develop a plan that fits your unique church. Through basic principles, case studies, and worksheets, McBride leads you through twelve logical steps for organizing and administering a small-groups ministry.

McBride, Neal F. *How to Lead Small Groups* (NavPress, 1990).
Covers leadership skills for all kinds of small groups—Bible study, fellowship, task, and support groups. Filled with step-by-step guidance and practical exercises to help you grasp the critical aspects of small-group leadership and dynamics.

Bible study methods

Braga, James. *How to Study the Bible* (Multnomah, 1982).
Clear chapters on a variety of approaches to Bible study: synthetic, geographical, cultural, historical, doctrinal, practical, and so on. Designed to help the ordinary person without seminary training to use these approaches.

Fee, Gordon, and Douglas Stuart. *How to Read the Bible for All Its Worth* (Zondervan, 1982).
After explaining in general what interpretation and application are, Fee and Stuart offer chapters on interpreting and applying the different kinds of writing in the Bible: Epistles, Gospels, Old Testament Law, Old Testament narrative, the Prophets, Psalms, Wisdom, and Revelation. Fee and Stuart also suggest good commentaries on each biblical book. They write as evangelical scholars who personally recognize Scripture as God's Word for their daily lives.

Jensen, Irving L. *Independent Bible Study* (Moody, 1963), and *Enjoy Your Bible* (Moody, 1962).
The former is a comprehensive introduction to the inductive Bible study method, especially the use of synthetic charts. The latter is a simpler introduction to the subject.

Wald, Oletta. *The Joy of Discovery in Bible Study* (Augsburg, 1975).
Wald focuses on issues such as how to observe all that is in a text, how to ask questions of a text, how to use grammar and passage structure to see the writer's point, and so on. Very helpful on these subjects.